STRAIGHT
FROM THE
EARTH

D0473513

STRAIGHT FROM THE EARTH

IRRESISTIBLE VEGAN RECIPES FOR EVERYONE

WITHDRAWN

Myra Goodman and Marea Goodman

Photographs by Sara Remington

CHRONICLE BOOKS

SAN FRANCISCO

Text copyright © 2014 by Myra Goodman and Marea Goodman.
Photographs copyright © 2014 by Sara Remington.
All rights reserved. No part of this book may be reproduced in any form
without written permission from the publisher.

Library of Congress Cataloging-in-Publication Data:
Goodman, Myra.
 Straight from the earth : irresistible vegan recipes for everyone /
 by Myra Goodman and Marea Goodman ; photographs by Sara Remington.
    pages cm
 Includes index.
 ISBN 978-1-4521-1269-5

1. Vegan cooking. 2. Cooking (Natural foods) 3. Cooking (Vegetables)
4. Earthbound Farm (Firm) I. Goodman, Marea. II. Title.

 TX837.G655 2014
 641.5'636—dc23

                    2013026597

Manufactured in China

Designed by Brooke Johnson
Prop styling by Sarah Cave
Food styling by Constance Pikulas
Food preparation by Chelsey Bawot
Camera assistance by Kassandra Medeiros
Typesetting by David Van Ness

10 9 8 7 6 5 4 3 2 1

Chronicle Books LLC
680 Second Street
San Francisco, California 94107
www.chroniclebooks.com

This book is dedicated to our family.
With gratitude to the generations that came before us
and love for generations to come.

WELCOME
To the Organic
HERB
GARDEN
SNIPS and TIES
Are available at the
HERB TABLE

CONTENTS

INTRODUCTION

VEGAN FOOD FOR EVERYONE
MYRA

What a revelation it's been to write this cookbook. I am thrilled to have assembled so many tasty and tempting purely plant-based recipes, and to have done so in collaboration with my beloved daughter, Marea. Although I haven't become a vegan or given up foods I've always loved, I've learned that vegan food can offer tremendous abundance and variety to meat eaters, vegetarians, and vegans alike. With the introduction of these new recipes into my life, I feel better nourished, extra energized, and more joyful about food than ever before.

Although I grew up eating mostly processed foods and very little fresh produce, my diet has been very healthy for the past twenty years. Living on our original two-and-a-half-acre organic farm (where we launched Earthbound Farm), I have had constant access to fresh organic produce. Because I eat a lot of salads, whole grains, and lean meats, I thought I couldn't do much better, so I was surprised by the riches and variety a plant-based diet had to offer.

When Marea and I decided to write a vegan cookbook, we began creating delicious and satisfying meals without a chicken breast or piece of steak at the center of the plate. Vegan means no animal products at all—no meat, fish, dairy, or eggs; not even honey (because it comes from bees). This project meant learning to utilize the vast selection of plant foods that come straight from the earth: fresh vegetables pulled from the soil or picked off the vine; sweet bush and tree fruit; the many tastes and colors of beans, peas, lentils, grains, and rice; and a huge variety of nuts and seeds.

Being so focused on personal and environmental health, I eat organic whenever possible. I've always known that I should eat fewer animal products, but until recently, I could never have imagined writing a vegan cookbook. I love meat and dairy, and was convinced that I needed to eat them in substantial quantities to feel satisfied. But then I started to notice that a lot of my favorite meals just happened to be vegan. The huge salad topped with roasted beets, beans, and pumpkin seeds from our farm stand; our delicious curry split pea soup; my pasta with heirloom tomato sauce—which my son refuses to sprinkle with Parmesan because he doesn't want to alter its perfect taste; the hummus and tomato sandwiches I rely on. It became clear to me that I was eating—and enjoying—a purely plant-based diet far more than I realized.

At the same time, Marea was in college at UC Berkeley, living in a co-op where many of the residents were vegan (Marea wasn't one of them). To make sure everyone could partake, none of the communal meals could contain any animal products whatsoever. Marea has always been a naturally confident and creative cook, but she didn't cook very often while living at home. Nonetheless, for her work shift she signed up with a friend to cook dinner every Sunday—for sixty people! Without too much planning, and using mostly ingredients regularly stocked in the co-op's fridge and pantry, they conjured up delicious multi-course meals every week. I was fascinated by the way Marea applied her creative mind and natural resourcefulness to come up with a whole array of wonderful new recipes.

I called Marea every Saturday, inevitably when she was busy and didn't have time to talk. But I just had to ask, "What are you making for dinner tomorrow?" And then Monday I had to check in: "How did it turn out?"

Most of their meals had an ethnic theme. One of Marea's favorites was a Thai dinner, complete with fresh spring rolls and delicious Thai coconut soup. Another night, their Vietnamese dinner earned them a standing ovation. I immediately begged her to come home and make that identical dinner for us. Not only was I proud, I was inspired.

A MOTHER-DAUGHTER COLLABORATION

Writing this cookbook together has highlighted the lifelong bonds we share and made us closer. Although Marea and I are alike in many ways, in other ways we are polar opposites. A clear example is our hair. I've had the same long hair my whole life with a length that has only varied by a few inches. Marea had long hair until she turned nineteen, when she cut it all off to see what short hair felt like. Next she experimented with a Mohawk, then shaved her head, and is now back to short hair. She's brave and confident enough to shake things up. And that goes for her cooking style as well, which is imaginative and bold, unencumbered by convention.

Initially, I worried that Marea's cooking style might be too unconventional for a cookbook. When she mentioned the ingredients in her Caesar salad dressing, my first reaction was "You *can't* put curry in a Caesar and still call it a Caesar!" That's me, the traditionalist. But then our family tried it for dinner, and we all agreed that it tasted fabulous. So we compromised: I could go with it if we could find an adjective to qualify "Caesar." After a lot of ideas that didn't quite capture its essence, Marea came up with the word "eccentric." Perfect—just like her salad. So there it is, Marea's "Eccentric Caesar Salad," right on page 61 of this book.

Most of Marea's recipes have a unique twist, and she applies that same imagination to my recipes. Marea loosens me up and inspires me to be more brave and adventurous.

She insisted on orange zest in my Banana Bread with Macadamia Nuts and Bittersweet Chocolate (page 33), which perfected the taste. She suggested spices I never would have thought of adding to my corn soup (see page 81)—coriander, paprika, and cayenne—taking it from very good to great. On the flip side, Marea loves really spicy and tart foods, so I've encouraged her to mellow her recipes so that they can appeal to a wider range of people. I beseeched her to reduce the vinegar in her Stuffed Mushrooms with Arugula, Walnuts, and Sun-Dried Tomatoes (page 102), and I had to restrain her from adding avocado to almost every recipe, including her Three-Berry Smoothie (page 43).

Many of the recipes in this book are true mother-daughter collaborations. Creating these recipes together pushed us both to new heights of enthusiasm and creativity. Coming up with new vegan recipes sparked my culinary imagination like never before. Fish tacos are a regular dinner at our house, so for this book I wanted to create a vegan version that would satisfy us. If I hadn't been looking for a fish alternative, I would never have come up with Plantain Tacos with Pureed Black Beans and Mango-Lime Salsa (page 155), a Caribbean-style dish that is out of this world. In the past, I added dairy to every smoothie, but now I'm enjoying our Tropical Green Smoothie (page 40) with a coconut water base. It's incredibly tasty, healthy, and refreshing. Marea and I both love falafels, but the sauce typically includes yogurt, so she invented a roasted cashew sauce that is amazingly delicious and makes our Baked Falafel Pitas (page 146) extra special.

Along the way, I had many more wonderful food discoveries. Marea introduced me to creamy, nutty hemp seeds, which make a great alternative to Parmesan on pasta dishes and salads—plus they are packed with healthy oils, protein, and

WHY I'M SO PASSIONATE ABOUT ORGANIC FOOD

When my husband, Drew, and I started Earthbound Farm thirty years ago, our decision to farm organically was pure instinct. We both grew up in New York City, and we didn't realize American agriculture was so reliant on chemicals until we landed on our little raspberry farm in California and got a crash course in the routine chemical applications from the departing farmer. Somehow we knew in our hearts that it had to be possible to grow food without any chemicals that were toxic enough to destroy weeds and insects. Nestled in the beautiful mountains of Carmel Valley, California, on two and a half acres packed with more than one hundred fruit and nut trees and the sweetest heirloom raspberries ever, our tiny farm felt like our own little Garden of Eden. We believed that what came straight from the earth—without any chemical interference—would be the healthiest food possible.

The growth of Earthbound Farm and the enormous explosion of the organic food movement has validated our instincts. Today, plenty of research has confirmed that there are many health benefits, especially for children, of eating food grown without synthetic agricultural chemicals. And the benefits to the environment are very significant as well. Organic farming protects our water supply and oceans, builds healthy soil, preserves biodiversity, and conserves natural resources.

Since organic food tastes wonderful, and organic farming keeps toxic chemicals out of our air, water, soil, and food supply, choosing organic is one of the best ways I can think of to care for my family and support a healthy planet. To learn more about organic food, see our Organic Food box on page 162.

SO MANY REASONS TO LOVE VEGAN FOOD

EATING VEGAN IS GREAT FOR YOUR HEALTH
Eating more fruits, vegetables, legumes, and whole grains—while reducing consumption of animal products—can lower your risk of developing diseases such as hypertension, heart disease, diabetes, arthritis, and many types of cancers.

EATING VEGAN IS ECONOMICAL
Beans, grains, and rice generally cost much less per calorie than meat and dairy, and since vegan dishes stay fresh longer than food made with animal products, you can cook in larger batches, and waste less food.

EATING VEGAN HELPS PROTECT THE ENVIRONMENT IN A BIG WAY
Every time you choose plant foods over meat and dairy, you're helping to reduce the global warming gases and water pollution generated by livestock production, and helping conserve water and natural resources.

EATING VEGAN HELPS ENSURE A HEALTHY FUTURE
Vegan food uses calories more efficiently. It takes 10 to 20 lb/4.5 to 9 kg of grain to make 1 lb/455 g of beef. Eating vegan also helps prevent overfishing and damage to ocean habitats and avoids the consumption of factory-farmed animals that are often raised inhumanely and routinely fed antibiotics and growth hormones.

EATING VEGAN IS DELICIOUS
The recipes in this book will prove that eating vegan can be a treat and not a sacrifice. If you're a skeptic, try our Very Chocolaty Chocolate Brownies (page 200)—the best brownies we've ever tasted!

iron. I learned about the benefits of coconut oil and the amazing properties of chia seeds. I realized that my use of butter and cheese was really habitual, and how easy it was to substitute different ingredients. I figured out how to make pancakes with flaxseed instead of eggs, and soymilk instead of cow's milk—pancakes that my son says are the best he's ever tasted! I grew to prefer my rich and flavorful Slow-Simmered Beans with Tuscan Kale on Bulgur (page 139) to pork chops or a hamburger.

I'm also thrilled that all vegan food is compostable; in fact, it stays fresh longer than food with animal products, so less is wasted. And I was ecstatic to realize I can eat my cookie dough without worrying about getting sick from raw eggs.

THE BENEFITS OF VEGAN FOOD

The vegan recipes we've created have enriched my understanding and appreciation of food straight from the earth—and all that the earth provides. These dishes are teeming with vitamins, minerals, and micronutrients. Plant foods are full of healthy fiber, while there is none in animal products. And we need to be concerned about cholesterol in animal products, but there is none in plant foods.

Many people wonder if vegan food can provide enough protein and other key nutrients like calcium and iron. To answer that question, we approached Ashley Koff, RD, a well-known dietitian who advised us and reviewed all the nutritional information in this book. She told us:

"There are two nutrition certainties: that a plant-based diet is the healthiest choice for you and for the environment, *and* that the quality of the food you put in your body matters. People will continue to debate which 'diet' is the healthiest—either from parts of the world (i.e. the Mediterranean, Japan, China, etc.) or what nutrients we should eat more or less of (carbs, protein, fats,

types of carbs, types of proteins, antioxidants, vitamins, minerals). But when one eats primarily plants, and especially a large variety of plants, it's proven that the body gets what it needs to develop, function, and repair as needed. The only nutrient not found in vegan food is B12, so that should be supplemented if you're eating a totally vegan diet."

As I began to run nutritional information on our vegan recipes, I was astonished at how loaded with nutrients they are—even most of the desserts. We're sharing this information at the end of every recipe because it's exciting to know that food so delicious also delivers so many health benefits. Although it's possible to be an unhealthy vegan (soda, candy, and most French fries are vegan, too), a diet focused on consuming a wide variety of whole, unprocessed plant-based foods is clearly the healthiest.

TASTE-TESTING WITH CARNIVORES

To see if our recipes could satisfy the pickiest carnivores, I asked Pam McKinstry to test many of them. Pam is a classically trained chef who relies heavily on eggs, dairy, and meat. She has authored eight cookbooks (including collaborating with me on my first two cookbooks), and frankly, she was a bit horrified when I asked if she would test recipes for a vegan cookbook. My biggest boost of confidence came when she reported back on our dishes. In her own words:

"My skepticism probably showed at the idea of working on a vegan cookbook, but I was astonished (along with my Irish husband, who is disappointed at any meal without meat) at how good everything tasted. Almost every recipe we trialed got rave reviews, and we never missed the meat. Best of all was the introduction to so many foods we had never eaten before. As a professional chef, it's embarrassing to admit that I've never cooked with coconut oil, hemp, flax or chia seeds, tempeh, or raw cashews. Now whole grains, legumes, nuts, and seeds will play a much more central role in my cooking."

Many people assume that eating plant-based meals regularly will be boring, and will increase their cravings for meat. My husband and I made those same assumptions. Drew loves throwing meat on the barbecue. When I started this book, he knew that the majority of our meals would be plant-based, and he was skeptical. He expected food that was strange, not tasty, and not filling enough. But because he is a wonderful husband, a committed environmentalist, and has the best palate in the family, he was willing to try.

This time, the surprise was on Drew. He didn't become a vegan, but he's definitely a convert. Here's what he says now:

"My expectations were so different from my experience. I really thought that the more I ate vegan food, the more I would crave animal products—but it's been the complete opposite. Now I want less meat and less often; it's become less appealing to me than it was. My whole eating pattern has shifted. I've become more mindful of what I eat and that makes me enjoy it more.

These are all dishes a true omnivore can eat without feeling as if you're sacrificing."

EVERYONE IS INVITED TO THE TABLE

I originally envisioned this book as a collection of "vegan recipes for omnivores," because I figured vegans had their food all figured out and only carnivores needed enticement. I had also assumed that since I eat animal products and my first two books contained recipes with meat, this cookbook might not be embraced by vegans. Another surprise! After vegan friends tried and loved these recipes, I happily expanded the concept to "vegan food for everyone."

Our goal in writing this cookbook is not to turn omnivores into vegans. Rather, it's to offer a diverse and delicious collection of recipes that makes choosing more plant-based meals too tempting to resist. "Vegan" has been a mysterious and slightly scary term to many people, and we want to demystify it—to let everyone know that eating vegan is a wonderful choice to make as often as possible.

When I observe the growing enthusiasm for vegan food, I always get a feeling of déjà vu, because this same transformation happened with

organic food. In 1984, when Drew and I started Earthbound Farm, organic food was considered strange, unappealing, hippie food. Now, thirty years later, "organic" stands for safe, delicious, high-quality food. Today we are beginning to see the same shift happen with vegan food, for many of the same reasons. Every time you choose something organic, or enjoy a mostly vegan meal instead of grilling up a big steak, you're making a positive impact on your health and helping to protect our planet.

These recipes also provide a great way to make food that can be enjoyed by friends and family who have varying diets. These recipes provide common ground, ideal for vegans and carnivores to eat together; they're perfect for a vegan to serve non-vegan guests and vice versa. Everyone is invited to the table!

WHAT YOU WILL FIND IN THIS BOOK

What you're holding in your hands is the result of more than a year of me and Marea passionately creating, testing, and recording our favorite vegan recipes—all of which passed the carnivore taste test. We hope this book will open the doors to vegan cooking for you—just like it did for us.

Here's some of what you'll find on these pages:

- Delicious and easy-to-make recipes organized into seven chapters, starting with breakfast and ending with dessert. We use only 100 percent whole grains in all our recipes—including our muffins, pancakes, breads, and pizza dough. We love the taste, the better nutrition, and the higher fiber.

- Nutritional information for every recipe, including calories, fat, carbohydrates, protein, and sodium, plus fiber, vitamins and minerals when they are present in significant amounts (10 to 19 percent of your daily requirement per

serving is considered a "good source" of a nutrient, while 20 percent and above is considered an "excellent source"). Just like a label on packaged food, the "Percent Daily Value" listed for our recipes indicates the percentage of the nutrients in one serving of food based on a 2,000-calorie-a-day diet. Additional factors, such as age and life stage, activity level, and health status, impact individual nutrient needs. For example, while an average-weight adult who is lightly active may need only 40 to 50 g of protein daily, a growing athlete could need as much as 80 to 90 g.

- Every chapter includes one in-depth box that highlights a type of food that is especially relevant to plant-based diets. We cover soy, seeds, nuts, legumes, grains, coconuts, and organic food. These boxes provide a lot of useful information, including nutritional highlights, directions for toasting nuts and seeds, cooking instructions for beans, how to make nut and seed milks, the benefits of choosing organic food, and much more

Finally, in the appendices, you'll find the following additional information:

- Eleven theme menu ideas perfect for special occasions, such as Middle Eastern Spread, Thanksgiving Feast, and Vegan Valentine (page 216)

- A conversion chart that shows the cup and gram yields for various chopped produce items we use in our recipes, and also an explanation of what we mean by different cutting terms— e.g., how big is a "medium dice"? (see page 217)

- The Environmental Working Group's chart of carbon footprints for different foods (see page 218)

MY ROOTS, MY PASSION

MAREA

I'm lucky: I grew up with the land. While a lot of American children ordered fast food for dinner, I was fed baby greens in my high chair and taught to garden. So many of our family's home videos highlight my brother's and my educational training in the garden, trying with all our concentration to correctly pronounce the words: "cawots," "poe-tae-toes," "celawy." We learned that tomatoes and corn grow in the summer, and that raspberries are best picked straight from the vine. We learned that it really is good to eat our broccoli.

I spent a lot of time with my mom in the kitchen. As soon as I got old enough, I helped her chop vegetables for dinner. Many nights I took on the role of her sous-chef. Although I was a faithful helper, my mom was really most proud of the way I could eat. As a mother who *loves* to feed her family, she often boasted about her small daughter's enormous appetite and joyfully watched me clean my plate. Needless to say, cooking and eating was, and is, a central part of our family's connection.

When I was in college, I moved into a vegan co-op. We sourced all our food from local and organic farms and ate most of our meals communally. It was there that I really learned to cook. Once a week, I prepared a meal for dozens of people, with only whole, plant-based ingredients. Cooking for that many every week, I learned to get creative. I learned that raw kale becomes deliciously digestible when massaged with something acidic like lemon juice or vinegar. I learned to use nutritional yeast for its satisfying cheese-like flavor, and to experiment with surprising spices. I learned, most importantly, the amazing joy of sharing food with friends.

After my junior year of college, I took some time off to travel in South America. So many of my favorite memories from that trip revolve around delicious foods and the cultures that revealed themselves to me through flavor. Every time I had the privilege of eating a meal with someone in their home, I learned more and more about the culture and the people of the places I visited. I got to know Brazil through the amazing fragrances of vegetables simmering in spicy coconut milk and the sticky texture of jackfruit on my fingers. Argentina's dedication to drinking *yerba mate* (a caffeinated infused beverage) became a practice I brought home. Even while I was traveling from place to place, never staying anywhere for too long, I got to relax into the grounding fact that, well, everybody eats. There is a special power in food, the way it brings people together, and the way that it can make even the most transitory traveler feel at home.

Food is still a central part of my life. I find solace in my kitchen, chopping onions and zucchini, meditating on magic combinations of herbs and spices. I worship garlic. My friends know me as The Feeder—I relish every "yes" to the question "Are you hungry?" because, like my mom, I love to help people feel full. I'm not a strict kitchen-dweller, however. Sometimes I'll get takeout Thai food or a quick burrito on the go. But even on those days when I feel too tired to cook for myself, my intimate relationship with food doesn't wane. I stay connected to the joy and the vital importance of eating.

This book has been an opportunity to express my love of food. In these pages, I have synthesized the experiences of the little girl who grew up pulling carrots out of tender earth with those of the young adult who learned to cook creatively for big groups of friends.

This book is also a special convergence of my mother's and my distinctive cooking styles and personalities, and a tribute to the intergenerational connection made available through food in my family. How special is it that I get to write a cookbook with the woman who fed me so generously for the first part of my life? Our mother-daughter connection is the pulse of this cookbook and is, definitely, the main reason I feel so connected to food. With this project, I hope to also extend a piece of myself to my future children and the generations to come.

This cookbook is by no means a prescription for how to eat. It is an invitation to indulge in your own creative expression of preparing, eating, and sharing whole, fresh ingredients. I hope that you make these recipes your own by adding a dash of your personality to every meal you prepare. Like me, I hope you grow to love these recipes with all your heart.

OUR COOKING TIPS

We are not professionally trained chefs. It's our love of food, our access to great ingredients, and our fearlessness that have enabled us to grow confident enough to share our recipes. We both have a simple style of cooking and are comfortable improvising and substituting. Over time, we've learned a few things to help make our cooking more enjoyable, healthful, and consistently delicious. Here are some tips we'd like to share:

BAKING

Vegan baking was scary at first, but it has become our favorite way to bake. Instead of using eggs, we use healthy chia and flaxseed (see page 70); instead of milk, we use soymilk, and we make it into a buttermilk substitute by adding lemon juice. The results are delicious and far healthier than typical baked goods. Two important baking tips (vegan or otherwise) are:

Ensure correct oven temperatures: Check your oven temperature with an oven thermometer, which is inexpensive and available anywhere that kitchen supplies are sold (including most large supermarkets). It turns out my oven runs 40 degrees cold, and Marea's 25 degrees hot. We discovered this only after our cooking times for the same recipes varied so much. Now we know to adjust the temperatures to compensate. We both test our ovens regularly.

Measure flour correctly: All the recipes in this book provide flour measurements by both the volume and weight. Weighing your flour ensures you are using the correct amount. However, if you are measuring by volume, the most accurate method is to fill a measuring cup by the heaping spoonful and then level it off with a knife or spatula. If you scoop out flour with a measuring cup, it will be dense and weigh up to 20 percent more, which can have a big impact on a recipe.

KITCHEN EQUIPMENT

Besides the basics like mixing bowls, pots and pans, a blender, etc., there are a few kitchen items we were slow to adopt that we encourage you to consider.

A kitchen scale: Weighing food is the most accurate way to get quantities correct. Digital scales are affordable and frequently come in very handy.

Good knives: If possible, invest in at least three good knives and keep them sharp. You will enjoy cooking so much more when you have a variety of high-quality knives that feel good in your hand (a nice wooden cutting board is important, too!). We suggest the following:

- A chef's knife with a 7- to 9-in/17- to 23-cm blade
- A paring knife with a 3- to 4-in/7.5- to 10-cm blade
- A serrated knife with a 9- to 10-in/23- to 25-cm blade

An ice cream maker: Ice cream makers are increasingly affordable and simple to use. It's amazing to discover how delicious homemade sorbets and ice creams are. Once you get going, it's easy to experiment with countless different flavors. The great recipes in this cookbook are a good enough reason to purchase one!

A spice grinder or coffee grinder: It takes less than a minute of your time to fresh-grind spices, and you'll taste the difference in the brighter flavors compared to preground spices in a jar. We also call for ground chia seeds for our brownies and ground flaxseed for our hot cereal and many baked goods.

Cast-iron skillets: We're huge fans of cast-iron skillets and truly adore ours. Cast iron is affordable and lasts forever. Food rarely sticks, and you don't need to worry about scratching off the nonstick surface as with Teflon pans. We can turn the heat up high to give food a nice crust, pop the skillet in the oven, and serve from it to keep food warm. It cooks evenly and beautifully. If you only buy one, get one that's 12 in/30.5 cm in diameter. Many of our recipes call for a skillet that's "preferably cast iron."

HOMEMADE STOCK

If you have never made your own stock, we urge you to try it at least once. Homemade vegetable stock tastes so much better than any packaged options, plus it's very economical, ecological, and easy. You can use up leftover bits of vegetables and ingredients like leek tops that would otherwise go to waste, and there is no packaging to throw away. Vegan stock is much quicker to make than meat stocks. Simmering for just 1 hour will make a flavorful enough stock. Make sure to use good-tasting water, though. If the water from your tap tastes metallic, it will affect the final product. See page 76 for our Easy Vegetable Stock recipe.

CHOOSING THE BEST OILS

Cooking oils can be made from seeds, fruits, nuts, and vegetables. Many commercial conventional cooking oils have been exposed to high temperatures, solvents, and chemical preservatives, and many oil sources—canola, corn, and soybeans in particular—are almost always genetically modified. The more you learn about the processes and additives involved in the manufacture of commercial oils, the more choosing organic makes sense. Although organic oils are more expensive, there are no GMOs, solvents, or preservatives involved in organic production, so they are your safest bet.

Oils have different smoke points, which is an important consideration in cooking. The smoke point is the temperature at which oils begin to

MAKE COOKING FUN

STAY RELAXED IN THE KITCHEN
Use your time in the kitchen as *your* time. Play your favorite music—relax, dance, enjoy. Embrace your creative inner chef and have fun.

CLEAN WHILE YOU COOK
Cooking is much more fun when you know you won't have tons of cleanup afterward, so clean while you cook. If your soup is simmering, wash up the knife and cutting board you used for prep. A little cleaning as you go will make a huge difference.

LET YOUR SENSES GUIDE YOU
Use these recipes as a guide for creating meals that suit your unique taste buds. Don't be afraid to change spices, sweetness, or presentation. Feel free to make any recipe more *you*.

smoke, and smoking oil releases unhealthy carcinogenic free radicals. Refined oils such as peanut, soybean, safflower, sunflower, avocado, or grapeseed are ideal for high-temperature cooking because they have very high smoke points, in the range of 440 to 520°F/227 to 270°C. Other oils such as extra-virgin olive oil, canola, and many nut oils have lower smoke points and are best used for lower-temperature cooking. Oils such as hemp seed, flaxseed, and some toasted nut oils should not be heated at all, but are ideal when used as flavor accents or nutrition enhancers.

Refined oils are typically colorless, odorless, and fairly flavorless. The cleanest oils are cold-pressed or expeller-extracted in a heat-controlled environment so that temperatures do not exceed 120°F/48°C. Unrefined oils have robust flavors and aromas, and they also are richer in nutrients. The only drawback is that unrefined oils have lower smoke points than their refined counterparts. As a general guide, choose unrefined oils for flavor and nutritional benefits. Choose refined oils that have been manufactured without chemicals or preservatives for high-heat cooking. (For more information, visit www.spectrumorganics.com.)

Chapter 1
BREAKFAST

PECAN, PUMPKIN SEED, and CURRANT GRANOLA

I love granola and would write a cookbook with nothing but granola recipes if anyone would publish it. Granola is delicious for breakfast with soymilk and berries or by the handful as a sweet and satisfying snack any time. It's very easy to make, and every batch lasts a long time. This version is a new favorite. I love the crispy pumpkin seeds, and there are so many currants in 1 cup that every bite is sure to have some. You can use this recipe as your base to experiment with other flavors. Keep the quantity of maple syrup and canola oil the same, but vary the dry ingredients any way you want, as long as they combine to measure 7 cups/770 g (excluding the dried fruit, which is always added after the granola has finished cooking, but before it's cool). Try any kind of nut, chopped or whole, and any type of seed. Play with the spice choices and quantities. Replace the currants with raisins, chopped dried apricots, or dried cherry pieces. The possibilities are endlessly delicious!   —MYRA

Makes about 8 cups/880 g

4 cups/460 g old-fashioned rolled oats

2 cups/240 g raw, unsalted pecans, coarsely chopped

1 cup/140 g raw, unsalted pumpkin seeds

1 tbsp plus 1 tsp cinnamon

½ tsp powdered ginger

½ tsp ground nutmeg

1 cup/240 ml maple syrup

⅓ cup/75 ml canola oil

1 cup/160 g currants or raisins

Position a rack in the center of your oven and preheat it to 325°F/ 165°C/gas 3.

Put the oats, pecans, pumpkin seeds, cinnamon, ginger, and nutmeg in a large bowl and mix to combine. Pour the syrup and oil over the dry ingredients and mix thoroughly (I like to use my hands).

Spread the mixture evenly in a large (about 12-by-17-in/30.5-by-43-cm) rimmed baking sheet and bake for 20 minutes.

Remove the pan from the oven and stir the granola thoroughly with a spatula, taking care to make sure all the granola by the edges and in the corners is well blended to avoid burning. Bake for another 10 minutes. Remove, stir, and return it to the oven for 10 more minutes.

The granola is ready when it's golden brown, fragrant, and dry. If it's not ready after the first 40 minutes of baking, return it to the oven and continue to check on it frequently, stirring every 5 minutes, until it's ready. Granola will burn quickly once it's cooked.

As soon as the granola is done, remove from the oven and sprinkle the currants over the top. Stir to combine.

Place the baking sheet on a cooling rack and let the granola cool completely before storing it in a plastic bag or airtight container. It will stay fresh at room temperature for about 4 weeks, and in the freezer for months.

½ CUP/55G: CALORIES: 360 | FAT: 21G | CARBS: 37G | PROTEIN: 8G | SODIUM: 0MG | DIETARY FIBER: 20% | IRON: 15% | COPPER: 10% | ZINC: 10%

PATCH

Original
Heirloom
Red
Raspberries

AMAZING GRAINS HOT CEREAL

This is my favorite breakfast cereal. It's delicious, sweetened mostly with dates and apples, and packed with fiber, protein, and healthy omega-3s. It takes a bit longer to cook than most packaged multigrain cereals where the grains have been cut, but I think it's well worth it to get the satisfying chew of the whole barley and rice. It reheats quickly in the microwave, so leftovers are super fast. —MYRA

Serves 6

½ cup/100 g pearled barley, rinsed

½ cup/100 g short-grain brown rice, rinsed

1 tsp salt

½ cup/85 g quinoa, thoroughly rinsed

½ cup/60 g old-fashioned rolled oats

½ cup/75 g chopped dried and pitted dates (about 10)

1 apple, peeled, medium dice

1 tbsp maple syrup

1½ tsp ground cinnamon

TOPPINGS

Walnut pieces, toasted (see page 117)

Ground flaxseed

Maple syrup or brown sugar (optional)

Milk or milk alternative (optional)

Pour 4½ cups/1 L of water into a large saucepan and add the barley, rice, and salt. Cover the pan and bring the mixture to the start of a boil over medium-high heat. Reduce the heat to low and simmer for 15 minutes, stirring occasionally.

Add the quinoa, oats, and dates and simmer, covered, for 15 minutes, stirring occasionally.

Stir in the apple, syrup, and cinnamon and simmer, covered, for an additional 5 minutes, stirring occasionally. Stir, remove the pan from the heat, and let the cereal sit, covered, for 5 minutes before serving.

Serve it sprinkled with toasted walnuts and ground flaxseed. If you like your cereal sweeter, add additional maple syrup or brown sugar. It's delicious with or without milk. Let any leftover cereal cool slightly; refrigerate it, covered, for up to 5 days. It reheats well in the microwave.

1 SERVING | NO TOPPINGS: CALORIES: 250 | FAT: 2G | CARBS: 54G | PROTEIN: 7G | SODIUM: 390MG | DIETARY FIBER: 28% | THIAMIN: 15% | VITAMIN B$_6$: 10% | IRON: 10% | COPPER: 10% | PHOSPHORUS: 15% | MAGNESIUM: 20%

BLUEBERRY CORNMEAL PANCAKES

When I first served my son these delicious pancakes, he asked me twice (with a lot of skepticism) if they were truly healthy. How is that possible when they taste so delicious? I told him they are all whole grain, with heart-healthy flaxseed, soymilk, and canola oil, plus antioxidant-rich blueberries and nutritious pecans. If you go light on the syrup, this is a legitimately healthy meal. At our house, we eat pancakes as an after-dinner snack more often than as a breakfast, and during the summer we almost always turn these into raspberry pancakes with the berries from our yard. It's a great recipe for experimenting with different fruit and nut combinations. In this recipe, we use the pecans as a topping, but they are also delicious folded right into the batter with the berries. In the winter, try thinly sliced apples or slices of bananas. It's hard to go wrong with these pancakes!   —MYRA

Serves 4 to 6; makes twelve 4-in/10-cm pancakes

1⅓ cups/315 ml plain, unsweetened soymilk, plus extra if the batter needs thinning

1 tbsp plus 1 tsp fresh lemon juice

2 tbsp ground flaxseeds

¼ cup/60 ml very hot water (about 180°F/82°C)

¼ cup/60 ml canola oil

1⅓ cups/185 g whole-wheat pastry flour

⅔ cup/100 g cornmeal

2 tbsp granulated sugar

1 tbsp baking powder

½ tsp salt

2 cups/280 g blueberries, plus 2 cups/280 g for serving (optional)

1 cup/120 g pecans, toasted (see page 117) and coarsely chopped

Confectioners' sugar (optional)

Pure maple syrup

In a large mixing bowl, whisk together the soymilk and lemon juice. Let the mixture sit for 5 to 10 minutes to thicken into "buttermilk."

In a small bowl, stir together the ground flaxseeds with the hot water. Allow to sit for 5 to 10 minutes until it thickens (this is our egg substitute).

Add the flaxseed mixture and oil to the bowl with the "buttermilk" and whisk to combine.

In a medium mixing bowl, whisk together the flour, cornmeal, granulated sugar, baking powder, and salt. Stir the dry ingredients into the wet ingredients until just combined, and then fold in the blueberries. If the batter is too thick to pour, thin it with a little more soymilk.

Heat a cast-iron skillet or nonstick griddle over medium heat. When the pan is hot, brush it with a thin layer of oil. Spoon a scant ¼ cup/60 ml of batter onto the griddle for each cake. This should spread to form a 4-in/10-cm pancake. Attempt to evenly distribute the berries in every pancake. Cook for approximately 2 minutes, until the batter begins to bubble and the bottoms are golden brown. Flip the pancakes and cook an additional minute or so, until the bottoms are golden brown. Repeat with the remaining batter. Top the pancakes with a sprinkle of the pecans, additional blueberries, and a dusting of confectioners' sugar, if desired. Serve with pure maple syrup.

2 PANCAKES (INCLUDES BLUEBERRY AND NUT TOPPING, NO SYRUP): CALORIES: 470 | FAT: 27G | CARBS: 54G | PROTEIN: 10G | SODIUM: 210MG | DIETARY FIBER: 40% | VITAMIN C: 20% | VITAMIN E: 15% | THIAMIN: 25% | RIBOFLAVIN: 10% | NIACIN: 15% | VITAMIN B$_6$: 10% | CALCIUM: 15% | IRON: 15% | COPPER: 25% | PHOSPHORUS: 40% | MAGNESIUM: 25% | ZINC: 15%

QUINOA-BANANA SKILLET BAKE

Banana and coconut lovers, this is for you. This is one of my most unique and tasty recipes and a great way to enjoy the health benefits of quinoa. This dish is a perfect choice for breakfast, although I can eat it any time of day. With the natural sweetness of bananas and dates, and a scoop of Creamy Coconut Ice Cream (page 209), you have just created a yummy dessert.   —MYRA

Serves 6

4 tbsp/60 ml coconut oil

1 cup/170 g quinoa, thoroughly rinsed

2 cups/480 ml very hot water (about 180°F/82°C)

¼ tsp salt

3 medium bananas, diagonally sliced

½ cup/75 g chopped dates

¼ cup/20 g shredded unsweetened coconut

3 tbsp brown sugar

2 tsp ground cinnamon

1 cup/110 g walnuts, toasted (see page 117) and coarsely chopped

Position a rack in the lower third of the oven and preheat it to 375°F/190°C/gas 5.

Warm 2 tbsp of the oil in a medium saucepan over medium heat. Add the quinoa and stir well to coat the grains. After 3 minutes, add the hot water and salt. Raise the heat to high and bring it to a boil. Reduce the heat to low and simmer, covered, for 10 minutes.

Meanwhile, heat the remaining 2 tbsp oil in a 9-in/23-cm cast-iron skillet (or oven-safe, nonstick pan). Add the bananas and cook over medium heat for 2 to 3 minutes, turning to brown on both sides. It may be necessary to do this in batches. Transfer the bananas to a plate and reserve. Set the skillet aside for later use.

After the quinoa has cooked for 10 minutes, add the dates, coconut, half of the sautéed bananas, 1 tbsp of the sugar, and 1 tsp of the cinnamon. Stir well and remove the pan from the heat. Pour the quinoa mixture into the reserved skillet and spread evenly.

Combine the walnuts and the remaining 1 tsp cinnamon and 2 tbsp sugar in a small bowl and stir to blend. Scatter the mixture over the quinoa, and spread evenly to cover. Arrange the remaining cooked bananas atop the nut mixture. Bake, uncovered, for 20 minutes, until the top is golden brown and fragrant. Serve hot, warm, or at room temperature.

1 SERVING: CALORIES: 450 | FAT: 26G | CARBS: 53G | PROTEIN: 8G | SODIUM: 105MG | DIETARY FIBER: 28% | POTASSIUM: 17% | THIAMIN: 15% | RIBOFLAVIN: 10% | VITAMIN B$_6$: 25% | FOLATE: 20% | IRON: 15% | COPPER: 30% | PHOSPHORUS: 25% | MAGNESIUM: 30% | ZINC: 10%

TOFU-VEGGIE SCRAMBLE

This protein-packed dish is my ideal breakfast for those mornings when I wake up hungry and have a long day ahead. The scramble is seasoned perfectly and is colored a nice yellow by the turmeric. This recipe contains a whole bunch of dino (Tuscan) kale—which is arguably the healthiest food on this planet—along with juicy chunks of mushrooms, bell pepper, garlic, and onion. It's a breakfast that will definitely fuel your body for whatever your day has in store. —MAREA

Serves 4

¼ cup/60 ml canola oil

1 small yellow onion, small dice

1 medium red onion, small dice

5 large garlic cloves, thinly sliced

2 red bell peppers, small dice

3 cups/180 g cremini mushrooms, trimmed and cut into bite-size pieces

14 oz/400 g firm tofu, crumbled

1½ tsp turmeric

1 tsp pure chipotle chile powder

Salt

¼ tsp ground ginger

Pinch of cayenne pepper

Pinch of red pepper flakes

3½ cups/105 g packed, trimmed, and thinly sliced dino (Tuscan) kale

1 tbsp toasted sesame oil

Freshly ground black pepper

½ cup/45 g thinly sliced green onions for garnishing

Place the oil in a very large skillet over medium-high heat. When the oil is hot, add the yellow and red onions and garlic. Cook, stirring frequently, until the onions are slightly translucent and fragrant, about 3 minutes. Add the bell peppers and cook for another 8 minutes. Reduce the heat to medium and add the mushrooms. Cook, stirring occasionally, until the mushrooms have softened, 6 to 8 minutes.

Reduce the heat to medium-low and add the tofu, turmeric, chipotle chile, 1 tsp salt, ginger, cayenne, and red pepper flakes. Cook, covered, for 10 to 15 minutes to allow the flavors to meld, stirring occasionally. Add the kale and cook, covered, stirring occasionally, until the kale is tender, 3 to 5 minutes.

Remove the skillet from the heat and stir in the sesame oil. Season with salt and pepper, garnish with the green onions, and serve immediately.

1 SERVING: CALORIES: 350 | FAT: 24G | CARBS: 22G | PROTEIN: 15G | SODIUM: 650MG | DIETARY FIBER: 20% | POTASSIUM: 24% | VITAMIN A: 80% | VITAMIN C: 90% | VITAMIN E: 20% | RIBOFLAVIN: 25% | NIACIN: 20% | VITAMIN B_6: 20% | FOLATE: 25% | CALCIUM: 30% | IRON: 20% | COPPER: 30% | PHOSPHORUS: 25% | MAGNESIUM: 20%

SWEET SIMMERED CINNAMON-ORANGE TOFU *and* BROWN RICE

I love starting my day with this filling and flavorful breakfast that's fast and easy to make. Simply simmer the tofu and leftover brown rice in soymilk, flavor it with cinnamon, fresh blood orange juice, maple syrup, and raisins. Then top it off with some chopped toasted hazelnuts, and savor every bite. It's OK to use regular oranges, or even ready-made fresh orange juice; I just love the reddish tone and tart taste of blood oranges. The texture is similar to that of hot cereals, but this dish is reminiscent of rice pudding, one of my favorite desserts. Each serving has 13 grams of protein, so it should keep you satisfied until lunchtime. I always cook my brown rice with salt, so if your leftover rice doesn't have any, you might consider adding a small pinch to the recipe while it's simmering.   —MYRA

Serves 3

1 tbsp canola oil

8 oz/225 g firm tofu, medium dice

1 cup/240 ml plain, unsweetened soymilk

2 cups/320 g cooked brown rice (see facing page)

1 tsp ground cinnamon

¼ cup/40 g raisins, very coarsely chopped

Juice of 2 small blood oranges or ¼ cup/60 ml fresh orange juice

2 tbsp pure maple syrup

TOPPING

3 tbsp chopped hazelnuts, toasted (see page 117)

Heat the oil in a medium saucepan over medium heat. Add the tofu and sauté for 5 minutes, stirring regularly.

Add the soymilk and rice and bring them to a simmer. Cook for 5 minutes, covered, stirring regularly. Most of the liquid should be absorbed.

Sprinkle the cinnamon over the mixture and stir to combine. Stir in the raisins, orange juice, and syrup. Cook uncovered for 2 minutes, stirring frequently. Remove the mixture from the heat and let it sit, covered, for 1 minute.

Serve it hot, sprinkled with 1 tbsp hazelnuts.

1 SERVING: CALORIES: 400 | FAT: 14G | CARBS: 58G | PROTEIN: 13G | SODIUM: 40MG | DIETARY FIBER: 20% | POTASSIUM: 16% | VITAMIN C: 20% | VITAMIN E: 10% | THIAMIN: 20% | NIACIN: 10% | VITAMIN B$_6$: 15% | IRON: 15% | COPPER: 20% | PHOSPHORUS: 20% | MAGNESIUM: 25% | ZINC: 15%

EASY BROWN RICE

Brown rice is a favorite side dish in our house. Leftovers heat quickly, and are a great addition to breakfast, lunch, or dinner. This recipe can be easily doubled or tripled.

Makes 3 cups/480 g

1 cup/200 g brown rice (short or long grain, rinsed or not rinsed)

2 tsp extra-virgin olive oil

½ tsp salt

Combine 2 cups/480 ml water with the rice, oil, and salt in a medium pot. Bring them to a boil over high heat. Reduce the heat to maintain a simmer, cover, and cook for 40 minutes without stirring.

Check to be sure all the water is absorbed. (If it's not, allow it to cook for a few more minutes, until all the water is absorbed.) Fluff with a fork, and allow the rice to rest, covered, for 5 minutes before serving.

½ CUP/80 G: CALORIES: 150 | FAT: 5G | CARBS: 23G | PROTEIN: 2G | SODIUM: 580MG | DIETARY FIBER: 8% | THIAMIN: 8% | NIACIN: 8% | VITAMIN B$_6$: 8% | PHOSPHORUS: 8% | MAGNESIUM: 10%

CRISPY POTATO *and* TEMPEH STIR-FRY

I absolutely love this breakfast. Simple to make and so satisfying, it is a morning favorite. Using unpeeled baby potatoes, protein-packed tempeh, onions, garlic, and some special spices, this stir-fry fills me up and keeps me going for a long time. It's a perfect recipe to bring to a potluck brunch, and often I double it (using two skillets) so that I can feed lots of hungry people. This is a delicious and healthy meal to eat on a Sunday morning when you're craving a belly full of hearty food.   —MAREA

Serves 4

1 lb/455 g baby Ruby Red or Yellow Finn potatoes, unpeeled

2 bay leaves

¼ cup/60 ml high-heat oil, such as safflower

1 small yellow onion, medium dice

8 oz/225 g tempeh, medium dice (see page 45)

3 large garlic cloves, thinly sliced

1½ tsp dried thyme

1 tsp sweet paprika

Pinch of ground nutmeg

Salt

Freshly ground black pepper

Put the potatoes and bay leaves in a medium pot and add enough water to just cover the potatoes. Cover the pot and cook over high heat until the potatoes are tender (but not mushy) when pierced with the tip of a knife, 15 to 25 minutes, depending on the size of the potatoes. Drain and rinse the potatoes in cold water, reserving the bay leaves. When cool enough to handle, cut the potatoes into ½-in/12-mm dice. If the potatoes are very wet, spread them on a clean kitchen towel and let them dry for 15 minutes.

Put the oil in a very large (at least 12-in/30.5-cm) skillet (preferably cast iron) set over medium-high heat. When the oil is hot, add the onion and cook, stirring frequently, until it softens, about 4 minutes. Add the tempeh and garlic and cook, stirring once or twice, until the tempeh begins to brown, 6 to 8 minutes.

Add the potatoes, reserved bay leaves, thyme, paprika, and nutmeg. Cook, stirring frequently, making sure to scrape the bottom of the pan, until the mixture has browned, 8 to 10 minutes. Remove the skillet from the heat and season with salt and pepper. Remove the bay leaves and serve immediately.

1 SERVING: CALORIES: 630 | FAT: 31G | CARBS: 69G | PROTEIN: 26G | SODIUM: 180MG | DIETARY FIBER: 24% | POTASSIUM: 40% | VITAMIN C: 40% | VITAMIN E: 15% | THIAMIN: 25% | RIBOFLAVIN: 30% | NIACIN: 30% | VITAMIN B_6: 50% | FOLATE: 15% | CALCIUM: 15% | IRON: 25% | COPPER: 50% | PHOSPHORUS: 40% | MAGNESIUM: 35% | ZINC: 20%

BANANA BREAD *with* MACADAMIA NUTS *and* BITTERSWEET CHOCOLATE

Is there anyone who doesn't love banana bread? This unusual version is scrumptious; it's very moist, with a tender crumb and lots of flavor. The addition of orange zest intensifies and complements the flavors of bananas, macadamia nuts, and chocolate. My family prefers the loaf shape for sweet breads, but since this loaf takes a full 80 minutes to cook, you can speed up the process by using a 9-by-9-in/23-by-23-cm pan, which cuts the cooking time in half. Topping this bread with a tablespoon of peanut butter adds extra protein and flavor for a wonderfully yummy start to your day. It's also a rich and satisfying treat any time. —MYRA

Serves 12

3 tbsp ground flaxseed

¼ cup plus 2 tbsp/90 ml very hot water (about 180°F/82°C)

1 cup/200 g packed light brown sugar

½ cup/120 ml melted coconut oil (see page 215)

1½ cups/220 g mashed ripe bananas (about 4 medium)

1 large orange, zested

2 cups/280 g whole-wheat pastry flour

2 tsp baking soda

¼ tsp salt

¾ cup/100 g chopped macadamia nuts

½ cup/75 g finely chopped bittersweet chocolate

Position a rack in the lower third of the oven and preheat it to 325°F/165°C/gas 3. Grease a 5-by-9-in/12-by-23-cm loaf pan or a 9-by-9-in/23-by-23-cm baking pan and set aside.

In a large mixing bowl, combine the flaxseed with the hot water. Allow to sit for 5 to 10 minutes until it thickens (this is our egg substitute).

Add the sugar and oil to the flaxseed mixture, whisking vigorously to combine. Whisk in the bananas and orange zest.

In a medium bowl, whisk together the flour, baking soda, and salt. Add the dry ingredients to the wet ingredients, stirring until just combined. Fold in the nuts and chocolate, and transfer the batter to the prepared pan.

If you are using a loaf pan, bake until the bread is golden brown and the top is firm to the touch, about 80 minutes. (Rotate the loaf after 50 minutes if your oven cooks unevenly.) If using a 9-by-9-in/23-by-23-cm pan, bake for 40 to 45 minutes, or until the edges pull away from the sides of the pan and a toothpick inserted into the center of the cake comes out clean.

Cool the banana bread in the pan on a wire rack for 5 minutes, and then turn it out onto the rack to finish cooling. Let cool at least 1 hour before cutting into 12 pieces. Store the bread at room temperature in plastic wrap or in a plastic bag. It will stay fresh for a good 3 days.

1 SLICE: CALORIES: 360 | FAT: 20G | CARBS: 47G | PROTEIN: 5G | SODIUM: 270MG | DIETARY FIBER: 20% | THIAMIN: 15% | VITAMIN B₆: 15% | PHOSPHORUS: 10% | MAGNESIUM: 15%

EVERYTHING HEALTHY BREAD

I grew up baking bread with my dad. On special days, we would devote hours to mixing, kneading, rising, and baking. He taught me the proper way to knead the dough, how it should feel when it's ready to be shaped into logs, and the perfect hollow sound it has when just out of the oven (he had a job as a baker in college and learned some good tricks). Baking bread is one of my favorite meditations. I love devoting half of my day to bread alchemy, letting the dough rise over and over again, and kneading until it is perfectly elastic. This bread is my version of the one we used to bake together. Adapted from *The Tassajara Bread Book* (the first cookbook my mom ever owned when she was younger than I am now), this recipe is a step-by-step guide to creating the best, most healthy bread you've ever baked. You can form the bread into two loaves or two rounds, or one of each (which is what I usually do). The total cooking time comes out to about 4 hours, but the amount of time you'll actually be working in the kitchen is less than 1 hour—most of the time is for letting the bread rise and bake.   —MAREA

Makes 2 loaves

1 tbsp active dry yeast

2 tbsp packed brown sugar

1 tbsp molasses

1 tbsp agave nectar

2 tbsp ground flaxseed

4 to 5 cups/520 to 650 g whole-wheat flour

½ cup/60 g old-fashioned rolled oats

½ cup/90 g millet

½ cup/70 g sunflower seeds, toasted (see page 72)

½ cup/70 g pumpkin seeds, toasted (see page 72)

½ cup/70 g sesame seeds, toasted (see page 72)

2 tbsp caraway seeds

¼ cup/60 ml olive oil

1 tbsp salt

Make a sponge (a wet, yeasty batter) by placing 3 cups/720 ml lukewarm water (85 to 105°F/30 to 40°C) in a very large mixing bowl and sprinkling it with the yeast. Stir gently with a large wooden spoon to dissolve. Add the sugar, molasses, and agave, and stir gently to dissolve. Add the flaxseed. Stir in 2½ cups/300 g of the flour, 1 cup/120 g at a time, stirring briskly after each addition. The mixture should be thick, but still loose enough to beat with a spoon. Beat the mixture briskly for about 30 seconds in a circular motion, making sure to stir through the middle of the mixture. The sponge should be very smooth.

Cover the bowl with a damp towel and set it in a warm, draft-free place. Let the sponge rise for 35 minutes, until it appears bubbly.

In a medium bowl, mix together the oats, millet, sunflower seeds, pumpkin seeds, sesame seeds, and caraway seeds. Set aside.

Uncover the sponge and pour the oil and salt over it. Mix them in by stirring around the side of the bowl and folding in toward the center, rotating the bowl with your other hand until completely incorporated. Add another 1 cup/120 g of flour and incorporate using the same folding method. Stir in the reserved seed mixture, 1 cup/120 g at a time. Continue to add flour in ¼ cup/30 g increments, until the dough comes away from the side of the bowl and forms a cohesive mass.

When it is impossible to continue stirring with a spoon, the dough is ready for kneading. This is a very important step: It creates heat that activates the gluten in the flour, which creates a lighter-textured bread.

Transfer the dough to a lightly floured surface. Stretch the dough by pressing down on it with your hands and body weight and rotating it frequently to ensure that all of it gets worked. Turn, fold, push, and repeat. If the dough sticks to the surface or your hands, add small amounts of flour to the dough and the kneading surface. As you work the dough, it will become more resistant, but increasingly elastic. Knead for 15 minutes.

Lightly oil a very large, dry bowl. Place the dough in the bowl, smooth-side down. Flip the ball of dough in the bowl to cover the other side with oil, leaving it crease-side down.

Cover the bowl with a damp towel and let it rise in a warm place until it has doubled in size, 50 to 60 minutes.

Punch down by gently pressing your fist into the dough, repeating this motion until the dough has been completely deflated. Cover and let it rise again until it has doubled in size, 40 to 50 minutes.

Generously oil two 8½-by-4-in/21.5 by 10 cm loaf pans, or a flat baking sheet if forming the dough into rounds. Set aside.

Turn the dough out onto a clean, dry surface lightly dusted with flour. If the dough is sticky, add more flour very sparingly. Knead lightly to form a round ball. With a sharp knife, cut the dough in half. Roll each piece into a log, squaring off the sides and ends, and pinching the seams together. Place each log in one of the prepared loaf pans, seam-side up. Flatten the dough with your fingers so that the bottom gets completely covered in oil. Then flip the dough over so the seam side is down, and push down with your fingers once again. Alternatively, form one or both pieces of dough into rounds, taking care to oil all sides. Cover the pans with a clean kitchen towel, set them in a warm, draft-free place, and let the dough rise until it has almost doubled in size, 20 to 30 minutes.

Meanwhile, position a rack in the middle of the oven and preheat it to 350°F/180°C/gas 4.

With a small, sharp knife, cut five ½-in-/12-mm-deep slits in the top of each loaf to help the bread bake evenly. Bake until the loaves are golden brown and have pulled away from the sides of the pan, 50 to 60 minutes. To test for doneness, turn a loaf out of the pan and tap the bottom, listening for a hollow sound. If the bread seems soft or doesn't sound hollow, continue baking a little longer and test again. Transfer the pans to a wire rack, and turn out the loaves. Let them cool on the rack for at least 45 minutes before slicing.

1 SLICE (12 SLICES IN A LOAF): CALORIES: 180 | FAT: 8G | CARBS: 26G | PROTEIN: 6G | SODIUM: 370MG | DIETARY FIBER: 20%

BLACKBERRY-BRAN MUFFINS

Bran muffins have always been one of my favorite treats, and I am thrilled that my vegan version can compete with the best muffins I've ever tasted. They are moist, not too dense, just sweet enough, and the bites of juicy blackberries make them extra special. Other berries work well, too. I always use this recipe to make olallieberry muffins when the berries are in season. The muffins freeze well and defrost on your counter in about 2 hours, or 20 seconds in the microwave. Lightly toasted, they taste almost as delicious as when they're freshly baked.   —MYRA

Makes 12 muffins

1 cup/240 ml plain, unsweetened soymilk

1 tbsp fresh lemon juice

2 cups/100 g wheat bran

½ cup/60 g old-fashioned rolled oats

2 tbsp ground flaxseed

¼ cup/60 ml very hot water (about 180°F/82°C)

¾ cup/150 g packed light brown sugar

½ cup/120 ml unsweetened applesauce

¼ cup/60 ml canola oil

1¼ cups/175 g whole-wheat pastry flour

1 tsp baking powder

1 tsp baking soda

½ tsp ground cinnamon

½ tsp salt

1 cup/130 g fresh blackberries

Position a rack in the lower third of the oven and preheat it to 350°F/180°C/gas 4. Lightly oil 12 muffin cups or line them with paper liners.

In a large mixing bowl, whisk together the soymilk and lemon juice. Let the mixture sit for 5 to 10 minutes to thicken into "buttermilk." Whisk the mixture and stir in the bran and oats.

In a medium mixing bowl, combine the flaxseed with the hot water. Allow to sit for 5 to 10 minutes until it thickens (this is our egg substitute). Whisk the sugar, applesauce, and oil into the flaxseed mixture. Add this mixture to the bowl with the bran, blending until the batter is combined.

In another medium mixing bowl, whisk together the flour, baking powder, baking soda, cinnamon, and salt. Add this mixture to the batter, stirring just until combined. Do not overmix. Carefully fold in the blackberries.

Fill each muffin cup with a heaping ⅓ cup/75 ml of batter. The muffin cups should be full and rounded at the top. Make an effort to divide the blackberries evenly among the muffins.

Bake for 35 to 40 minutes, or until the muffins are firm to the touch and a toothpick inserted into a muffin (avoiding the blackberries if you can) comes out clean.

Cool the muffins in the tin for 10 minutes. Turn out the muffins and continue to cool them on a wire rack for another 10 minutes before serving.

1 MUFFIN: CALORIES: 200 | FAT: 7G | CARBS: 35G | PROTEIN: 5G | SODIUM: 210MG | DIETARY FIBER: 32% | NIACIN: 10% | IRON: 10% | PHOSPHORUS: 20% | MAGNESIUM: 20%

MYRA'S BELOVED OATCAKES

I first discovered oatcakes at a little crumpet shop in Carmel. I used to eat them for breakfast several times a week, and I was practically heartbroken when the bakery closed more than a decade ago. So it is with great enthusiasm that I can report I've resumed my oatcake habit—and this recipe makes the best oatcakes I've ever tasted. They contain so many wholesome and delicious ingredients, I couldn't settle on a title. Should I call them "Orange, Cranberry, Coconut Oatcakes"? Maybe "Maple, Pecan, Cranberry Oatcakes"? Or "Whole-Grain Flax-Coconut-Cranberry Oatcakes"? So instead of singling out any ingredients, they became "Myra's Beloved Oatcakes."

These treats lie somewhere between a muffin and a granola bar; they are very dense and barely rise when they bake. For me, they are absolutely perfect as a breakfast or snack with a cup of hot tea. I also like to make them as thinner, crispier oat squares (directions for that variation follow). They're easy to transport, and eaten with peanut butter or almond butter, they'll keep you full—and satisfied—for a long time. If you, too, develop a serious oatcake habit, the recipe makes a generous amount; you can freeze them and thaw at room temperature in about an hour.   —MYRA

Makes 16 cakes

---

3 cups/345 g old-fashioned rolled oats

2 cups/280 g whole-wheat pastry flour

1 tsp salt

¾ tsp baking powder

¾ cup/180 ml maple syrup

½ cup/120 ml melted coconut oil (see page 215)

1 orange, zested and juiced, plus water to make ⅓ cup/75 ml

2 tbsp ground flaxseed

1 cup/120 g pecans, lightly toasted (see page 117) and coarsely chopped

1 cup/120 g dried cranberries

1 cup/80 g unsweetened shredded coconut

Preheat the oven to 325°F/165°C/gas 3 and generously grease 16 muffin cups.

In a large mixing bowl, stir together the oats, flour, salt, and baking powder.

In a medium bowl, combine the syrup, coconut oil, and orange zest.

In a small bowl, whisk together the orange juice and flaxseed. Add them to the wet ingredients, and whisk thoroughly to combine.

Mix the wet ingredients into the dry ingredients and stir until just combined.

Add the pecans, cranberries, and coconut. Mix together just until thoroughly blended (I find it's easier to do this with my hands because the batter is very stiff).

Fill each muffin tin with ½ cup/120 ml batter. Press down so the batter is lightly compact and the top is flat. The muffin cups should be close to full.

Bake for 25 to 35 minutes, until the tops are golden brown. Remove from the oven and cool them in the pan on a rack for 5 minutes. Turn out the oatcakes onto the rack and continue cooling for another 10 minutes. Serve them warm or at room temperature.

---

1 OATCAKE: CALORIES: 330 | FAT: 17G | CARBS: 40G | PROTEIN: 5G | SODIUM: 170MG | DIETARY FIBER: 24%

Variation: BELOVED OAT SQUARES

Oat squares are a slightly smaller version of my oatcakes, perfect for lunch boxes or a more modest treat any time of day. I often make a dozen oatcakes from the recipe, and then use a 7-by-5-in/17-by-12-cm baking dish for the remaining batter, which yields 6 oat squares.

Makes 24 squares

To make all the batter into squares, grease a 15-by-10-in/38-by-25-cm baking pan. Spread the batter out evenly. It should be about ½ in/12 mm thick. Bake about 25 to 35 minutes, until the surface is golden brown. Let cool on a rack for 5 minutes.

Cut into 24 squares, approximately 2½ by 2½ in/ 6 by 6 cm each. Let them cool in the pan for 5 minutes more, then carefully remove. Finish cooling them on a rack.

1 OAT SQUARE: CALORIES: 220 | FAT: 12G | CARBS: 27G | PROTEIN: 4G | SODIUM: 110MG | DIETARY FIBER: 16%

TROPICAL GREEN SMOOTHIE

Bananas, mango, and pineapple blend beautifully with coconut water and lime in this sensational smoothie (pictured at the back of the photo on page 42). Terri Nordby, who gave me this recipe, says this morning smoothie is her favorite way to include flaxseed in her daily diet. I made it optional since some people prefer a smoother texture. Even flaxseed-free, this drink is highly nutritious (see the nutritional information for both versions below). This smoothie also provides a perfect use for those ripe bananas that might never get eaten. —MYRA

Serves 2

12 oz/355 ml coconut water

2 cups/60 g packed spinach

1 ripe medium banana, fresh or frozen (peel and slice before freezing)

¾ cup/100 g frozen pineapple

½ cup/70 g frozen mango

2 pitted dates, cut into thirds

1 small or ½ large lime, zested and juiced

2 tbsp ground flaxseed (optional)

Combine the coconut water and spinach in a blender, and blend until smooth.

Add the banana, pineapple, mango, dates, lime zest and juice, and flaxseed, if using. Pulse until the big chunks of fruit are broken up, and then blend until very smooth, about 1 minute. Serve immediately.

1 SERVING (WITH FLAXSEED): CALORIES: 200 | FAT: 4G | CARBS: 40G | PROTEIN: 5G | SODIUM: 200MG | DIETARY FIBER: 32% | POTASSIUM: 26% | VITAMIN A: 60% | VITAMIN C: 70% | THIAMIN: 15% | RIBOFLAVIN: 15% | VITAMIN B$_6$: 20% | FOLATE: 20% | IRON: 10% | COPPER: 15% | PHOSPHORUS: 10% | MAGNESIUM: 30%

1 SERVING (WITHOUT FLAXSEED): CALORIES: 150 | FAT: 0.5G | CARBS: 37G | PROTEIN: 3G | SODIUM: 200MG | DIETARY FIBER: 24% | POTASSIUM: 24% | VITAMIN A: 60% | VITAMIN C: 70% | RIBOFLAVIN: 10% | VITAMIN B$_6$: 15% | FOLATE: 20% | MAGNESIUM: 20%

PEANUT BUTTER–BANANA SMOOTHIE

If you love peanut butter and bananas, you'll be very happy with the combination in this delicious smoothie (pictured on the center left of the photo on page 42). This recipe proves that it's not hard to get enough protein on a plant-based diet. With 17 grams in each serving, this smoothie has more protein than two eggs (minus any cholesterol). It's sweetened only with bananas and dates, which is exactly sweet enough for me. If you have a sweet tooth, you might want to use sweetened soymilk instead of unsweetened, or add a splash of agave nectar. This recipe takes only a few minutes to make, but do remember to freeze the bananas and chill the soymilk ahead of time.   —MYRA

Serves 2

2 cups/480 ml plain unsweetened soymilk, chilled

2 ripe medium bananas, frozen (peel and slice before freezing)

3 tbsp all-natural peanut butter (crunchy or smooth)

4 pitted dates, each cut into 3 pieces

Combine the soymilk, bananas, peanut butter, and dates in a blender. Pulse on the "chop" speed until the bananas are broken up, and then on the highest speed for about 1 minute, until the smoothie is completely blended. Serve immediately.

1 SERVING: CALORIES: 370 | FAT: 17G | CARBS: 46G | PROTEIN: 17G | SODIUM: 60MG | DIETARY FIBER: 40% | POTASSIUM: 27% | VITAMIN C: 15% | VITAMIN E: 10% | NIACIN: 20% | VITAMIN B_6: 30% | FOLATE: 10% | IRON: 15% | COPPER: 10% | PHOSPHORUS: 10% | MAGNESIUM: 20%

THREE-BERRY SMOOTHIE

This smoothie (pictured at the front of the photo on the facing page) is an ideal summer treat. Freezing bananas and berries is a great way to rescue fruit that is starting to turn, and they make this smoothie icy cold without diluting the flavor with ice cubes. However, if you don't have frozen fruit, you can substitute 1 cup/240 ml of the nut milk with 1 cup/240 ml crushed ice. You can use either almond, hazelnut, or soymilk for this recipe—experiment with the flavors you like best. Served with a sprig of fresh mint in each glass, this rich fruity drink is bound to satisfy your senses.   —MAREA

Serves 4

2 ripe medium bananas, fresh or frozen (peel and slice before freezing)

2 cups/480 ml almond, hazelnut, or soymilk

1 cup/120 g frozen raspberries

1 cup/130 g frozen strawberries, chopped

1 cup/130 g frozen blueberries

⅛ tsp vanilla extract

4 sprigs fresh mint for garnishing

Combine the bananas, almond milk, raspberries, strawberries, blueberries, and vanilla in a blender and puree until smooth. Pour the smoothie into four glasses and garnish each with a sprig of fresh mint. Serve immediately.

1 SERVING: CALORIES: 170 | FAT: 3G | CARBS: 33G | PROTEIN: 5G | SODIUM: 65MG | DIETARY FIBER: 24% | POTASSIUM: 14% | VITAMIN C: 50% | VITAMIN B_6: 20% | FOLATE: 10% | COPPER: 15% | MAGNESIUM: 15%

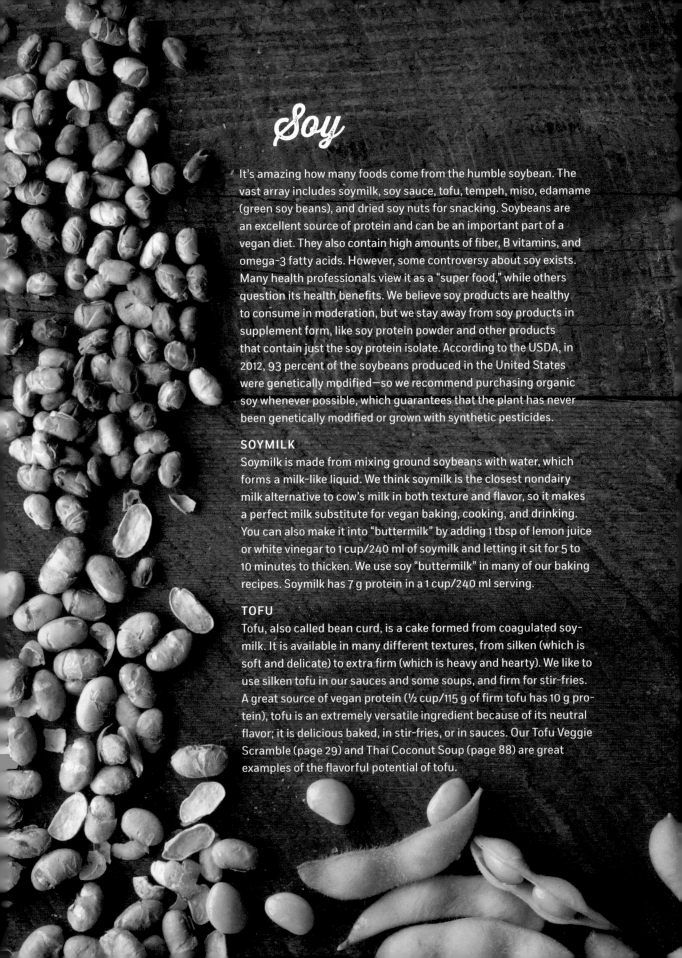

Soy

It's amazing how many foods come from the humble soybean. The vast array includes soymilk, soy sauce, tofu, tempeh, miso, edamame (green soy beans), and dried soy nuts for snacking. Soybeans are an excellent source of protein and can be an important part of a vegan diet. They also contain high amounts of fiber, B vitamins, and omega-3 fatty acids. However, some controversy about soy exists. Many health professionals view it as a "super food," while others question its health benefits. We believe soy products are healthy to consume in moderation, but we stay away from soy products in supplement form, like soy protein powder and other products that contain just the soy protein isolate. According to the USDA, in 2012, 93 percent of the soybeans produced in the United States were genetically modified—so we recommend purchasing organic soy whenever possible, which guarantees that the plant has never been genetically modified or grown with synthetic pesticides.

SOYMILK

Soymilk is made from mixing ground soybeans with water, which forms a milk-like liquid. We think soymilk is the closest nondairy milk alternative to cow's milk in both texture and flavor, so it makes a perfect milk substitute for vegan baking, cooking, and drinking. You can also make it into "buttermilk" by adding 1 tbsp of lemon juice or white vinegar to 1 cup/240 ml of soymilk and letting it sit for 5 to 10 minutes to thicken. We use soy "buttermilk" in many of our baking recipes. Soymilk has 7 g protein in a 1 cup/240 ml serving.

TOFU

Tofu, also called bean curd, is a cake formed from coagulated soymilk. It is available in many different textures, from silken (which is soft and delicate) to extra firm (which is heavy and hearty). We like to use silken tofu in our sauces and some soups, and firm for stir-fries. A great source of vegan protein (½ cup/115 g of firm tofu has 10 g protein), tofu is an extremely versatile ingredient because of its neutral flavor; it is delicious baked, in stir-fries, or in sauces. Our Tofu Veggie Scramble (page 29) and Thai Coconut Soup (page 88) are great examples of the flavorful potential of tofu.

TEMPEH

Tempeh is a dense cake made from whole fermented soybeans. It's an excellent source of protein (1 cup/130 g of cooked tempeh has about 30 g protein) and is easier to digest than other soy products, because the fermenting process produces good bacteria (like probiotics), which help balance bacteria to help promote a healthy digestive system. (And a healthy digestive system contributes to better overall health, energy, and immune function.) Tempeh shines in our delicious Butternut Squash, Black Bean, and Kale Tamales with Spicy Tomatillo Salsa (page 161) and our Crispy Potato and Tempeh Stir-Fry (page 32).

MISO

Miso is a thick paste made from fermented soybeans. It is relatively high in protein (each 2 tbsp serving contains 4 g). Salty and flavorful, miso is a wonderful ingredient in soups and sauces—such as our Miso-Roasted Eggplant (page 180).

SOY SAUCE

Soy sauce is a liquid made from fermented soybeans that adds delicious flavor to stir-fries and soups. In our book, we usually choose low-sodium soy sauce, because you can always add salt but you can't take it away. Also make sure to find soy sauce that contains no MSG. Try our recipe for Teriyaki Tofu Broccolette on Wild Rice (page 133) for a creative way to make a delicious teriyaki sauce with soy sauce.

SOYBEAN OIL

Organic soybean oil has many health benefits: It is rich in polyunsaturated fatty acids like omega-3 and -6, and it also contains high amounts of vitamin E. For cooking, use soy oil for up to medium-high heat (360°F/182°C).

Chapter 2

SALADS

GRILLED HEARTS OF PALM SALAD *with* GRAPEFRUIT *and* AVOCADO

When my dad and I were in Argentina a few years ago, we made the most amazing culinary discovery: *grilled* hearts of palm. Resting on a bed of fresh, peppery wild arugula, the warm, savory hearts of palm lit up our taste buds. This salad is my attempt to re-create that experience. Served with a delicate orange and olive oil vinaigrette and topped with grapefruit and avocado, these grilled hearts of palm are well supported by many vibrant flavors. —MAREA

Serves 4

AGAVE VINAIGRETTE

½ cup/120 ml extra-virgin olive oil

3 tbsp apple cider vinegar

1 tsp agave nectar, plus more as needed

½ tsp orange zest

Pinch of salt

Freshly ground black pepper

SALAD

14 oz/400 g can or jar of whole hearts of palm

1 tbsp plus 1 tsp extra-virgin olive oil

5 oz/140 g baby arugula

1 grapefruit, segmented (see Note)

1 ripe avocado, thinly sliced

To make the vinaigrette: Combine the oil, vinegar, agave, zest, salt, and pepper in a small jar. Seal the lid tightly and shake vigorously until emulsified. Taste, and add more agave if desired. Shake vigorously once more, then set aside at room temperature.

To make the salad: Cut each of the hearts of palm in half lengthwise. Let them dry, flat-side down, on a paper towel.

In the meantime, place a grill pan or skillet over medium-high heat. With a pastry brush, spread 1 tbsp of the oil over the pan. When the pan is hot, carefully arrange the hearts of palm, flat-side down, so that the ribs are perpendicular to the ridges. With a pastry brush, brush the tops of the hearts of palm with the remaining 1 tsp oil. Cook until the grill marks are golden brown, about 5 minutes. Remove the hearts gently with tongs, or turn off the grill and let it cool for a few minutes.

Toss the arugula with ⅓ cup/75 ml of the vinaigrette. Add more if desired. Divide the arugula evenly among four salad plates. Arrange a quarter of the grapefruit segments, avocado, and hearts of palm on each of the plates. Drizzle with some of the remaining dressing, and serve immediately.

NOTE: SEGMENTING CITRUS FRUIT
Cut the top and bottom ends off of the fruit so that it can stand level on your cutting surface. With a sharp knife, cut downward, following the contour of the fruit, removing the peel and the pith. Then, slice between each white membrane of the fruit to release the flesh in segments, discarding the tough membrane.

1 SERVING: CALORIES: 290 | FAT: 25G | CARBS: 17G | PROTEIN: 5G | SODIUM: 510MG | DIETARY FIBER: 28% | POTASSIUM: 18% | VITAMIN A: 20% | VITAMIN C: 70% | VITAMIN B₆: 10% | FOLATE: 30% | CALCIUM: 15% | IRON: 20% | COPPER: 15% | PHOSPHORUS: 10% | MAGNESIUM: 20% | ZINC: 10%

RASPBERRY SALAD *with* BABY GREENS *and* RASPBERRY–GOLDEN BALSAMIC VINAIGRETTE

My husband, Drew, calls this the "Earthbound Farm Heritage Salad" because it combines both crops that launched Earthbound Farm: raspberries and spring mix. These two ingredients come together beautifully in this delightful salad, and they are perfectly complemented by creamy avocado, sweet, crunchy pecans, and a red-tinged raspberry–golden balsamic vinaigrette. The special vinegar is made by mixing some raspberries with vinegar, letting it sit, and then straining it. Easy, unique, and delicious! —MYRA

Serves 4

RASPBERRY–GOLDEN BALSAMIC VINAIGRETTE

2 cups/240 g raspberries

¼ cup/60 ml golden balsamic vinegar

⅓ cup/75 ml extra-virgin olive oil

⅓ cup/75 ml toasted pecan oil or toasted walnut oil

1 tsp Dijon mustard

½ tsp salt

Freshly ground black pepper

SALAD

5 oz/140 g spring mix

1 ripe avocado, cut into bite-size pieces

½ cup/60 g raw, unsalted pecans, toasted (see page 117) and coarsely chopped

To make the vinaigrette: In a small bowl, combine ½ cup/60 g of the raspberries with the vinegar. Mash the berries with a fork until they have thoroughly blended with the vinegar. Allow them to sit for 20 to 30 minutes, and then strain the mixture through a fine-mesh sieve, pressing with a fork to release all the juices. Discard the seeds. You should have approximately ⅓ cup/75 ml vinegar.

Place the olive and pecan oils, mustard, salt, pepper, and the raspberry vinegar in a glass jar and seal the lid tightly. Shake the jar vigorously to combine.

To make the salad: Toss the spring mix with ½ cup/120 ml of the dressing. Taste and add more if desired. Divide the greens among four salad plates and top each serving with some of the avocado, pecans, and the remaining raspberries. Serve immediately.

1 SERVING: CALORIES: 560 | FAT: 55G | CARBS: 18G | PROTEIN: 4G | SODIUM: 370MG | DIETARY FIBER: 36% | VITAMIN A: 40% | VITAMIN C: 60% | IRON: 15% | COPPER: 15%

CRESS, BELGIAN ENDIVE, PERSIMMON, *and* HAZELNUT SALAD

I love sweet and fragrant Fuyu persimmons. When they're in season from October through December, I cut them into little bites and toss them into salads. With their vibrant color and juicy firm texture, they are a terrific complement to greens that have a little bite. Although toasted hazelnuts will work just fine, try our Double-Roasted Maple-Spiced Hazelnuts for a unique autumn salad that's as pretty as it is tasty.   —MYRA

Serves 6

WHITE WINE VINAIGRETTE

¾ cup/180 ml extra-virgin olive oil (or half olive oil and half pecan oil)

¼ cup/60 ml white wine vinegar

1½ tsp Dijon mustard

Salt

Freshly ground black pepper

SALAD

3 heads Belgian endive (about 4 oz/115 g each)

2 bunches watercress, leggy stems removed

2 Fuyu persimmons, peeled, cored, small dice

¾ cup/105 g hazelnuts, toasted (see page 117) or Double-Roasted Maple-Spiced Hazelnuts (page 111), coarsely chopped

To make the vinaigrette: Put the oil, vinegar, and mustard in a jar. Seal the lid tightly and shake to combine. Season with salt and pepper. Keep at room temperature while you prepare the salad.

To make the salad: Trim the bottom ends of the endives and remove any damaged outer leaves. Cut the endives crosswise into ¼-in-/ 6-mm-thick slices, discarding any of the solid cores. You should have about 3 cups/300 g.

Just before serving, place the endive and watercress in a large bowl and add half of the dressing. Toss to combine, adding more dressing as desired. Divide the salad among six plates, and top each serving with some of the persimmons and hazelnuts. Serve immediately.

1 SERVING (WITH TOASTED HAZELNUTS): CALORIES: 390 | FAT: 39G | CARBS: 15G | PROTEIN: 3G | SODIUM: 140MG | DIETARY FIBER: 20% | VITAMIN A: 35% | VITAMIN C: 25% | THIAMIN: 10% | COPPER: 15%

SPINACH SALAD *with* MAPLE-ROASTED BUTTERNUT SQUASH *and* WALNUTS

This is a special salad. I love the colorful and flavor-packed combination of warm cubes of roasted butternut squash, crunchy bits of red onion, and the nutty sweetness of pecans, all served on a bed of baby spinach. Tossing the butternut squash and pecans in maple syrup before roasting imparts a slight sweetness, which is nicely balanced by the red wine vinaigrette. —MYRA

Serves 4

RED WINE VINAIGRETTE

½ cup/120 ml extra-virgin olive oil

2 tbsp plus 2 tsp red wine vinegar

1 garlic clove, crushed

1 tsp Dijon mustard

Salt

Freshly ground black pepper

SALAD

2 cups/280 g butternut squash, peeled, medium dice

1 tbsp plus 1 tsp olive oil

1 tbsp plus 1 tsp pure maple syrup

Salt

Freshly ground black pepper

½ cup/60 g pecans, coarsely chopped

5 oz/140 g baby spinach

½ medium red onion, thinly sliced

To make the vinaigrette: Combine the oil, vinegar, garlic, and mustard in a small jar. Seal the lid tightly and shake vigorously until emulsified. Season it with salt and pepper. Set aside at room temperature.

To make the salad: Position a rack in the middle of the oven and pre-heat it to 400°F/200°C/gas 6.

In a medium bowl, toss the squash with 1 tbsp of the oil and 1 tbsp of the syrup. Sprinkle with ½ tsp salt and a pinch of pepper. Spread the squash in a single layer on one end of a rimmed baking sheet. Roast it for 20 minutes, or until the cubes begin to lightly brown, stirring after 10 minutes, and keeping the cubes in a single layer.

Meanwhile, toss the pecans with the remaining 1 tsp oil and 1 tsp syrup and add a pinch of salt. After the squash has roasted for 20 minutes, remove the baking sheet from the oven and add the pecans to the pan, keeping them separate from the squash at the opposite end of the pan. Reduce the oven temperature to 300°F/150°C/gas 2. Cook for 10 minutes, stirring the nuts once.

Remove the baking sheet from the oven, and let the squash and nuts cool for a few minutes while you assemble the salad.

Place the spinach in a large bowl and add ⅓ cup/75 ml of the vinai-grette, tossing to coat the greens. Taste and add more dressing, as desired. Divide the spinach among four salad plates. Top each serving with a quarter of the onion, squash, pecans, and a sprinkling of pepper. Serve immediately.

1 SERVING: CALORIES: 470 | FAT: 43G | CARBS: 22G | PROTEIN: 4G | SODIUM: 350MG | DIETARY FIBER: 24% | POTASSIUM: 13% | VITAMIN A: 150% | VITAMIN C: 25% | THIAMIN: 15% | VITAMIN B$_6$: 10% | FOLATE: 25% | IRON: 15% | COPPER: 15% | MAGNESIUM: 15%

RED LEAF, JICAMA, and ORANGE SALAD with CITRUS-SESAME-SOY VINAIGRETTE

Earthbound Farm's executive chef, Sarah LaCasse, made this wonderful salad for a lunch meeting one day. After I sheepishly had a huge third helping, and then confirmed the recipe "just happened to be vegan," I knew it was meant for this cookbook. The dressing is a wonderful combination of quintessential Asian ingredients—soy, sesame, and ginger—sweetened with fresh orange juice and agave. The jicama is juicy and crunchy, adding a nice texture to the salad. Sarah's original salad had equal parts red leaf lettuce, baby spinach, and arugula, so you might want to give that combination a try, too.   —MYRA

Serves 4

CITRUS-SESAME-SOY VINAIGRETTE

3 tbsp canola oil

3 tbsp toasted sesame oil

3 tbsp soy sauce or tamari sauce

2 tbsp fresh orange juice

2 tbsp rice vinegar, brown or white

1 tsp grated peeled fresh ginger

1 tsp agave nectar

Pinch of freshly ground black pepper

SALAD

3 medium heads red leaf lettuce, torn into bite-size pieces

2 medium oranges, segmented (see Note, page 48)

1 cup/120 g matchstick pieces jicama

½ small red onion, cut in half through the stem end and thinly sliced

2 tbsp sesame seeds, toasted (see page 72)

To make the vinaigrette: Combine the canola oil, sesame oil, soy sauce, orange juice, vinegar, ginger, agave, and pepper in a small jar. Seal the lid tightly and shake vigorously. Let the dressing sit at room temperature if you are making the salad within 2 hours. Otherwise, refrigerate for up to 1 week, and let it return to room temperature before using.

To make the salad: Put the lettuce, orange segments, jicama, and onion in a large salad bowl. Toss with half of the dressing. Add the sesame seeds and toss again. Taste, and add more dressing if desired. Serve immediately.

1 SERVING: CALORIES: 310 | FAT: 23G | CARBS: 24G | PROTEIN: 4G | SODIUM: 810MG | DIETARY FIBER: 24% | VITAMIN A: 70% | VITAMIN C: 120% | VITAMIN E: 10% | THIAMIN: 10% | FOLATE: 10% | IRON: 25%

MIXED CHICORY SALAD *with* AVOCADO, GARLIC CROUTONS, *and* PINE NUTS

My husband often says he doesn't have enough chicory in his life, so in his honor, I created this salad featuring chicory's white color and crisp appeal. He calls it my "European bistro salad" and we enjoy it whenever we're lucky enough to find beautiful, well-blanched heads of escarole (ones with lots of white leaves in the center) or frisée at the market. The red wine vinaigrette has a strong Dijon mustard flavor to complement the slightly bitter greens. It goes especially well with the buttery pine nuts and croutons, which contribute a pleasing crunch to the dish. Slices of creamy avocado add a mellow note and a luscious soft texture to this delicious salad.   —MYRA

Serves 4

RED WINE VINAIGRETTE

¼ cup plus 2 tbsp/90 ml extra-virgin olive oil

2 tbsp red wine vinegar

2 tsp Dijon mustard

1 tsp crushed garlic

Salt

Freshly ground black pepper

SALAD

2 heads Belgian endive (about 4 oz/115 g each)

1 large head chicory (such as escarole or frisée)

1 head Treviso radicchio, sliced into bite-size pieces

1 large ripe avocado, thinly sliced

¼ cup/30 g pine nuts, toasted (see page 117)

1 cup/60 g Quick Garlic Croutons (facing page)

To make the vinaigrette: Combine the oil, vinegar, mustard, and garlic in a small jar. Seal the lid tightly and shake vigorously to emulsify. Season with salt and pepper and set aside at room temperature.

To make the salad: Trim the bottom ends of the endive and remove any damaged outer leaves. Cut the endive crosswise into ¼-in-/6-mm-thick slices, discarding any of the solid cores. You should have about 2 cups/200 g. Cut the bottom end off the chicory and remove the tough, dark green outer leaves. Frisée leaves can generally be left whole. Escarole leaves should be cut into bite-size pieces, about 1-in/2.5 cm wide. You should have about 3 cups/90 g of chicory.

In a large bowl, combine the endive, radicchio, and chicory and toss with half of the vinaigrette. Add more dressing as desired. Divide the greens among four plates, and top each salad with 4 or 5 avocado slices, 1 tbsp of pine nuts, and ¼ cup/15 g of croutons. Serve immediately.

1 SERVING (WITH CROUTONS): CALORIES: 380 | FAT: 33G | CARBS: 21G | PROTEIN: 6G | SODIUM: 220MG | DIETARY FIBER: 32% | POTASSIUM: 15% | VITAMIN C: 20% | THIAMIN: 15% | FOLATE: 20% | COPPER: 20% | MAGNESIUM: 15%

QUICK GARLIC CROUTONS

These croutons are very quick to make and are a great crunchy complement to both soups and salads. The bread can either be fresh or a few days old. Warning: They are so yummy they'll make it hard for you to go back to store-bought croutons! I've started doubling the recipe because my husband, Drew, can happily nosh on a whole batch.

Makes about 2½ cups/150 g

Nine ½-in/12-mm slices of a large baguette or 12 slices of a thin baguette

2 tbsp extra-virgin olive oil

1¼ tsp crushed garlic

Pinch of salt

Position a rack in the lower third of the oven and preheat it to 350°F/180°C/gas 4.

Toast the baguette slices very lightly in a traditional toaster or toaster oven. Allow to cool. Mix the oil, garlic, and salt together in a small bowl. With a pastry brush, brush both sides of the toast with this mixture, and then cut the slices into ½-in/12-mm cubes. Transfer the cubes to a rimmed baking sheet and bake until they are golden brown and crispy, 10 to 15 minutes, turning once. Allow to cool completely before using. Store any leftovers in an airtight container for up to 5 days.

¼ CUP/15 G: CALORIES: 70 | FAT: 3.5G | CARBS: 8G | PROTEIN: 2G | SODIUM: 90MG

COLORFUL GARDEN COBB SALAD *with* CREAMY AVOCADO DRESSING

This salad is spectacular. It combines eight colorful vegetables with garbanzo beans, sunflower seeds, and hemp seeds for protein and added nutrition. The extra-delicious creamy avocado dressing also happens to be one of my family's favorite vegetable dips. Because my husband and son like their salads heavily dressed, I always double the dressing recipe, which gives them plenty for the salad and extra for vegetable dipping. The salted sunflower seeds take only about 10 minutes to make, but you can skip this step by using plain seeds or packaged roasted and salted sunflower seeds. This recipe makes an extra-large salad, but you can always refrigerate some of the vegetables and greens for the next day. Just don't dress the salad or add the seed toppings until right before serving.   —MYRA

Serves 4 as an entree or 8 as an appetizer

CREAMY AVOCADO DRESSING

1 large ripe avocado

2 green onions, white bulb plus 2 in/5 cm of the green, sliced

1 large garlic clove, pressed

⅓ cup/75 ml extra-virgin olive oil

¼ cup/60 ml fresh lemon juice

¾ tsp salt

Pinch of cayenne pepper

To make the dressing: Put the avocado, green onions, and garlic in a blender or food processor. Process to a rough puree. Add the oil, lemon juice, salt, cayenne, and 3 tbsp cold water. Process until the dressing is smooth and creamy.

SALAD

2 romaine hearts, cut into bite-size pieces

4 cups/120 g packed baby spinach

2 cups/140 g thinly sliced red cabbage

2 cups/200 g coarsely grated carrots

1 small jicama, peeled and coarsely grated

2 cups/300 g pear or cherry tomatoes, cut in half lengthwise

1 medium cucumber, peeled, seeded, medium dice

1 yellow bell pepper, medium dice

1½ cups/420 g cooked garbanzo beans (drained and rinsed if canned)

½ cup/70 g Salted Sunflower Seeds (recipe follows)

¼ cup plus 2 tbsp/80 g hemp seeds

To make the salad: In a large salad bowl, combine the romaine, spinach, cabbage, carrots, jicama, tomatoes, cucumber, bell pepper, and garbanzo beans. Toss with the dressing. If serving the salad family-style, leave it in the large bowl and top with the hemp and sunflower seeds. Otherwise, divide the salad among individual plates, and top each serving with seeds. Serve immediately.

1 SERVING: CALORIES: 620 | FAT: 41G | CARBS: 53G | PROTEIN: 18G | SODIUM: 810MG | DIETARY FIBER: 76% | POTASSIUM: 43% | VITAMIN A: 290% | VITAMIN C: 200% | VITAMIN E: 30% | THIAMIN: 20% | RIBOFLAVIN: 20% | NIACIN: 20% | VITAMIN B₆: 35% | FOLATE: 90% | CALCIUM: 20% | IRON: 40% | COPPER: 30% | PHOSPHORUS: 25% | MAGNESIUM: 25% | ZINC: 15%

SALTED SUNFLOWER SEEDS

½ cup/70 g raw, unsalted sunflower seeds

1 tsp extra-virgin olive oil

½ tsp salt

Pinch of cayenne pepper

Position a rack in the lower third of the oven and preheat it to 350°F/180°C/gas 4.

Put the sunflower seeds, oil, salt, and cayenne in a small bowl and toss thoroughly with your fingers. Spread the seeds in a single layer on a rimmed baking sheet. Bake for 10 minutes, stirring once, until the seeds are fragrant and golden brown. Watch them closely to make sure they don't burn. Remove them from the oven and allow the seeds to cool completely before using. Store any leftovers in an airtight container for up to 2 weeks.

2 TBSP: CALORIES: 90 | FAT: 7G | PROTEIN: 3G | SODIUM: 290MG

ECCENTRIC CAESAR SALAD

When I created this Caesar salad, I did a silly dance around the kitchen. Seriously—it is that good. And the name is perfect for it. I'm betting that this Caesar salad dressing is like nothing you've ever tasted. It is extremely eccentric and undeniably delicious. Who would have thought that curry powder would be the perfect addition to a Caesar dressing? Not me before I took the risk of adding it—but now I am a total convert. And the nutritional yeast gives this dressing a cheese-like flavor that could please even the most omnivorous Caesar salad connoisseur. This recipe makes extra dressing that you can store in an airtight container in the refrigerator for up to 1 week. Topped with our Quick Garlic Croutons (page 57), capers, avocado, and hemp seeds, this dynamic salad will delight your adventurous taste buds. —MAREA

Serves 6

CAESAR DRESSING

½ cup/70 g raw cashews

3 tbsp extra-virgin olive oil

3 tbsp fresh lemon juice

3 tbsp nutritional yeast (see Note)

1 tbsp Dijon mustard

1 large garlic clove

¾ tsp salt

¼ tsp curry powder

Freshly ground black pepper

SALAD

2 large heads romaine lettuce, chopped or torn into bite-size pieces

2 cups/120 g Quick Garlic Croutons (page 57)

1 ripe avocado, medium dice

½ cup/65 g hemp seeds

⅓ cup/55 g capers

To make the dressing: Combine the cashews, oil, lemon juice, yeast, mustard, garlic, salt, curry powder, and pepper in a food processor and add ¼ cup plus 3 tbsp/75 ml warm water. Process until the mixture is very smooth, 2 to 3 minutes, scraping down the sides of the bowl once or twice.

To make the salad: Toss the romaine with ½ cup/120 ml of the dressing. Add more to taste if desired. Divide the lettuce among six plates, and top each with some of the croutons, avocado, hemp seeds, and capers. Serve immediately.

NOTE: NUTRITIONAL YEAST

Nutritional yeast has a delicious, savory, cheesy flavor that's especially welcome in many dairy-free recipes. It's also extremely nutrient dense, packed with amino acids, B-vitamins, folic acid, selenium, zinc, and many more important minerals. It gives our Caesar salad dressing a yummy, cheesy flavor, and we also love it sprinkled on popcorn, soups, beans, and pasta. Many people add it to vegetable juice to enhance the nutrition. It comes in both flake and powder form (we prefer the flakes for our recipes) and is available in natural food stores, both in bulk and in cans.

Note that nutritional yeast is different from baker's yeast, and it's also not the same as brewer's yeast (which is a by-product from the beer industry). Nutritional yeast is made from a single-celled organism called *Saccharomyces cerevisiae*, which is typically grown on molasses and then harvested, washed, and dried with heat to deactivate it. It should be stored in a cool and dry place in an airtight bag or container.

1 SERVING (USING ½ CUP OF DRESSING): CALORIES: 390 | FAT: 26G | CARBS: 30G | PROTEIN: 13G | SODIUM: 830MG | DIETARY FIBER: 32% | VITAMIN A: 80% | VITAMIN C: 40% | THIAMIN: 15% | RIBOFLAVIN: 10% | FOLATE: 35%

CABBAGE *and* CARROT CRUNCH SALAD

This salad is delicious to eat, beautiful to behold, and very healthful. It combines the crunch of red cabbage, carrots, succulent romaine hearts, crispy apples, and almonds—all complemented by sweet-tart dried cranberries and an agave-Dijon vinaigrette. You can make this salad any time of year, but I turn to it most often in the winter, because these tasty and highly nutritious ingredients are always available, even when the rest of produce selection has dwindled. When the days are cold, short, and gray, this salad brings a welcome pop of color and vibrancy to your table.   —MYRA

Serves 6

AGAVE-DIJON VINAIGRETTE

½ cup/120 ml extra-virgin olive oil

3 tbsp plus 1 tsp red wine vinegar

2 tbsp agave nectar

1½ tsp Dijon mustard

¼ tsp salt

Pinch of freshly ground black pepper

SALAD

1 large romaine heart, cut or torn into bite-size pieces

2 cups/140 g shredded red cabbage

2 large carrots, coarsely grated

1 large sweet-tart apple (such as Honey Crisp or Fuji), medium dice

½ cup/75 g raw, unsalted almonds, toasted (see page 117) and chopped

½ cup/60 g dried cranberries, coarsely chopped

1 tbsp plus 1 tsp finely chopped fresh spearmint (optional)

To make the vinaigrette: Combine the oil, vinegar, agave, mustard, salt, and pepper in a small jar. Seal the lid tightly and shake vigorously to emulsify. Set aside at room temperature.

To make the salad: Combine the romaine, cabbage, and carrots in a large bowl. Reserve 2 tablespoons of the vinaigrette. Add ½ cup/120 ml of the vinaigrette (or more as desired) to the vegetables, and toss to combine. Divide the salad among six plates or bowls.

Toss the apples with the 2 tbsp reserved vinaigrette and divide it among the individual salads. Top each salad with equal amounts of almonds, cranberries, and spearmint (if using). Serve immediately.

1 SERVING: CALORIES: 300 | FAT: 23G | CARBS: 23G | PROTEIN: 3G | SODIUM: 150MG | DIETARY FIBER: 16% | VITAMIN A: 100% | VITAMIN C: 45% | VITAMIN E: 15% | FOLATE: 15%

HEIRLOOM LETTUCE SALAD
with FRESH HERBS

This simple salad works well with almost any main dish for dinner, and it turns a bowl of soup and piece of crusty bread into a perfect lunch. The heirloom lettuce leaves are beautiful and succulent, but if you can't find any, feel free to substitute butter lettuce. The radishes contribute a pretty color and gentle bite, and the fresh herbs add wonderful flavor. This vinaigrette is one of my favorite salad dressings, so I like to double the recipe to have extra on hand. It stays fresh in the refrigerator for up to 2 weeks.   —MYRA

Serves 4

DIJON VINAIGRETTE

¼ cup plus 2 tbsp/90 ml olive oil

2 tbsp white wine vinegar

1 large garlic clove, pressed

2 tsp Dijon mustard

½ tsp salt

Pinch of freshly ground black pepper

SALAD

4 medium heads heirloom lettuces (assorted colors preferred, such as red and green oak leaf, red and green Bibb, tango, etc.) torn into bite-size pieces

2 cups/240 g thinly sliced radishes

½ cup/15 g chopped chives

½ cup/15 g packed very coarsely chopped flat-leaf parsley leaves

To make the vinaigrette: Combine the oil, vinegar, garlic, mustard, salt, and pepper in a jar. Seal the lid and shake vigorously to emulsify. Set aside at room temperature.

To make the salad: Combine the lettuces, radishes, and herbs in a large salad bowl. Toss with about two-thirds of the dressing and taste to see if more is needed. Serve immediately.

1 SERVING: CALORIES: 160 | FAT: 17G | CARBS: 4G | PROTEIN: 2G | SODIUM: 400MG | VITAMIN A: 100% | VITAMIN C: 60% | FOLATE: 15% | IRON: 20%

HEALTHY GREENS *with* CARROTS *and* PARSLEY

This easy recipe has become one of my favorites, and it was purely a product of serendipity. My family was hungry for a salad on a winter day when my fridge was almost empty. The only greens I had were baby kale, and my only vegetable was one huge carrot. We also had a bit of volunteer Italian flat-leaf parsley that survived the cold in our garden. I decided to cut the carrot into tons of very thin slices with a mandoline and combined the three ingredients into a salad, tossed with a white wine vinaigrette flavored with Dijon mustard and garlic. We were all surprised at how delicious it turned out. Now we've perfected it by adding baby spinach and salted sunflower seeds. If you don't want to spend the bit of time making our Salted Sunflower Seeds (page 59), it's fine to substitute preroasted and salted sunflower seeds, or just raw seeds if you prefer. If you can't find baby kale, use all baby spinach. This is a salad that makes you feel nourished and wonderfully healthy.   —MYRA

Serves 4

WHITE WINE VINAIGRETTE

¼ cup plus 2 tbsp/90 ml extra-virgin olive oil

2 tbsp white wine vinegar

1 tsp Dijon mustard

1 clove garlic, crushed

Salt

Fresh ground black pepper

SALAD

3 cups/90 g packed baby kale

2½ cups/75 g packed baby spinach

1½ cups/160 g very thinly sliced carrots (about 2 medium)

½ cup/15 g packed coarsely chopped flat-leaf parsley

½ cup/70 g Salted Sunflower Seeds (page 59)

To make the vinaigrette: Combine the oil, vinegar, mustard, garlic, ¼ tsp salt, and a big pinch of pepper in a glass jar and seal tightly. Shake vigorously until the dressing emulsifies. Adjust salt and pepper to taste.

To make the salad: Combine the kale, spinach, carrots, and parsley in a large salad bowl. Toss with about two-thirds of the dressing. Add more dressing to taste. Serve topped with the sunflower seeds.

1 SERVING: CALORIES: 270 | FAT: 25G | CARBS: 11G | PROTEIN: 5G | SODIUM: 310MG | DIETARY FIBER: 16% | POTASSIUM: 14% | VITAMIN A: 190% | VITAMIN C: 50% | VITAMIN B6: 10% | FOLATE: 25% | IRON: 10% | COPPER: 15% | PHOSPHORUS: 20% | MAGNESIUM: 10%

WHEAT BERRY, BABY KALE, GRAPE, *and* ORANGE SALAD

Baby kale is mild and convenient to use because the whole leaf is edible. If you can't find it, you can substitute full-size kale by removing the stem and slicing the leaf very thinly: ¼ in/ 6 mm wide and not longer than 2 in/5 cm. The wheat berries take a full hour to cook, and another 20 minutes or so to cool, but they can easily be cooked a day ahead of time. —MYRA

Serves 8

WHEAT BERRIES

2 cups/400 g wheat berries

1 tsp salt

CURRY-ORANGE VINAIGRETTE

⅔ cup/165 ml extra-virgin olive oil

¼ cup/60 ml golden balsamic vinegar

Zest of 1 orange

2 tbsp fresh orange juice

2 tsp agave nectar

1½ tsp Dijon mustard

1 tsp salt

¾ tsp curry powder

Pinch of cayenne pepper

Pinch of ground ginger

Freshly ground black pepper

SALAD

5 oz/140 g baby kale

1 cup/150 g seedless red grapes, halved

1 cup/150 g seedless green grapes, halved

2 oranges, segmented (see Note on page 48)

Salt

Freshly ground black pepper

1 cup/110 g raw, unsalted walnuts, toasted (see page 117) and coarsely chopped

To make the wheat berries: Rinse them and then put them in a medium pot with 6 cups/1.4 L water and the salt. Bring them to a boil, and then reduce to a simmer. Cook, covered, for 1 hour, until the wheat berries are just tender. Add a few cups of cold water to the pot, stir, and then strain. Place the wheat berries in a very large bowl to cool, stirring occasionally to help them along.

To make the vinaigrette: Combine the oil, vinegar, zest, juice, agave, mustard, salt, curry powder, cayenne, ginger, and pepper in a small jar. Seal the lid tightly and shake vigorously to combine. Set aside at room temperature.

To make the salad: Combine the cooled wheat berries with the kale in a large bowl. Toss with ½ cup/120 ml of the dressing. Add the grapes and orange segments and another ¼ cup/60 ml of the dressing and toss again. Add more dressing if desired, and season with salt and pepper. Toss in the walnuts right before serving.

1 SERVING: CALORIES: 480 | FAT: 32G | CARBS: 49G | PROTEIN: 8G | SODIUM: 480MG | DIETARY FIBER: 28% | VITAMIN C: 60% | IRON: 10% | COPPER: 15%

QUINOA TABBOULEH

Quinoa tabbouleh is a great variation of traditional Middle Eastern tabbouleh, which is made with bulgur wheat. The combination of fresh tomatoes, cucumber, tons of fresh parsley, and mint tossed with a lemon vinaigrette is irresistible. A side of quinoa tabbouleh is a great quick snack, and it turns a bowl of soup into a filling lunch. When served with our Three-Color Hummus (page 106), it makes a perfect Mediterranean-style appetizer. Salads with tomatoes are best eaten before they've been refrigerated, but this salad will be just fine for up to 5 days in the refrigerator. If you want to up the nutrition even more, serve the tabbouleh with a sprinkling of hemp seeds. —MYRA

Serves 8

QUINOA

1½ cups/255 g quinoa, thoroughly rinsed

½ tsp salt

LEMON VINAIGRETTE

¾ cup/180 ml olive oil

1 lemon, zested

¼ cup plus 1 tbsp/75 ml fresh lemon juice

2 large garlic cloves, pressed

¾ tsp salt

Pinch freshly ground black pepper

SALAD

2 large vine-ripe tomatoes, small dice

1 cucumber (preferably seedless, peeled if not), small dice

1½ cups/45 g packed finely chopped fresh flat-leaf parsley

⅔ cup/20 g packed finely chopped fresh spearmint

4 large green onions, white bulb and 2 in/5 cm of green, thinly sliced

Salt (optional)

Freshly ground pepper (optional)

To make the quinoa: In a medium pot, combine the well-rinsed quinoa with 3 cups/720 ml water. Bring to a boil over high heat and then reduce the heat to maintain a simmer. Simmer, covered, for 15 minutes, until all the water is absorbed. Add the salt. Fluff the quinoa and transfer it to a large bowl to cool, stirring occasionally.

To make the vinaigrette: Combine the oil, lemon zest and juice, garlic, salt, and pepper in a small jar. Seal the lid tightly and shake vigorously to combine. Set aside at room temperature.

To make the salad: Toss ¼ cup/60 ml of the dressing with the cooled quinoa. Add the tomatoes, cucumber, parsley, spearmint, and green onions to the quinoa. Pour on the remainder of the dressing, and toss until thoroughly combined. Season with additional salt and pepper if needed.

1 SERVING: CALORIES: 250 | FAT: 22G | CARBS: 14G | PROTEIN: 3G | SODIUM: 390MG | DIETARY FIBER: 12% | VITAMIN A: 35% | VITAMIN C: 60% | FOLATE: 15% | IRON: 15%

Seeds

We all know that good things come in small pack-ages—and that can hold true for what we eat as well. Seeds are versatile little gems packed with tons of nutrients. Most people are familiar with the trio of popular seeds: sesame, pumpkin, and sun-flower. But in this cookbook, we glorify three other seeds that are especially useful for vegan cooking: hemp, chia, and flax.

CHIA SEEDS

It might stretch your memory to recall that chia seeds were known to sprout hair for Chia Pets, but these days they are famous for their great nutritional profile. In every 1 oz/30 g serving, these tiny gems contain 42 percent of your daily value of fiber, 18 percent of your calcium, 4 g of protein, and gener-ous amounts of essential fatty acids. When stirred into liquid, they soften and absorb ten times their own weight of that liquid, which makes them ideal to use as a thickener, binder, and egg substitute in many types of recipes. Chia seeds come in both white and black varieties and can be found at your local natural foods store or online.

FLAXSEED

Flaxseed is well known for its health benefits—primarily because it is a terrific source of omega-3 fatty acids. In addi-tion, each 1 oz/30 g serving has 31 percent of your daily value of fiber, and 5 g of protein. To absorb its essential nutrients, it's important to grind flaxseed before eating it. Once ground, you can put flaxseed in a wide variety of dishes, from smoothies to cereals to salads. For cakes and cookies, we combine ground flaxseed with hot water to create a binding agent to replace eggs. Flaxseed is available at most grocery stores, ground or whole. Flax oil is also a delicious and healthy oil for salad dressings or raw sauces, but it shouldn't be heated. Ground flaxseed, or opened bags of preground flaxseed, must be stored in the refrigerator or freezer to prevent rancidity.

HEMP SEEDS

A true "super food," hemp seeds are packed full of omega-3 and -6 fatty acids and offer a diverse range of nutrients, including all of your essential amino acids. Hemp seeds have an amazing 11 g of protein in each 3 tbsp serving. They have a delicious nutty flavor and look similar to sesame seeds. Hemp seeds are a great addition to many baked goods, but our favorite way to eat them is sprinkled on salads. You can find hemp seeds at your local natural foods store, or order online. Once the package is opened, it's best to store them in the refrigerator. Hemp seeds also make great milk, which you can find in many grocery stores, or make at home (see page 72). They are generally sold already shelled.

PUMPKIN SEEDS

Prepare to be surprised: Pumpkin seeds, also known as *pepitas*, are a protein powerhouse—packing 8 g per 1 oz/30 g serving. They are also rich in key nutrients such as vitamin E, iron, magnesium, and zinc; they provide both essential and unsaturated fatty acids. Buy them in the shell, shelled, roasted, or raw.

SESAME SEEDS

Sesame seeds are extremely nutritious. A 1 oz/30 g serving has 5 g of protein and provides 27 percent of your daily value of calcium and 23 percent of iron. When toasted, their rich flavor and delicate crunch can provide the perfect finishing touch to many dishes, especially Middle Eastern and Asian cuisines. Toasted sesame oil is great for dressings and raw sauces, and raw sesame oil can be used for both medium- and high-heat cooking (350 to 445°F/180 to 230°C). Sesame seeds are also the primary ingredients in tahini.

SUNFLOWER SEEDS

Sunflower seeds supply a concentrated array of vitamins and minerals and an impressive 6 g of protein per 1 oz/30 g. Sunflower seeds can be ground into flour or butter, added to granola and snack bars, used as a garnish for vegetables or salads—or eaten right out of your hand. Raw sunflower oil is good for high heat cooking (445 to 460°F/230 238°C). We love sunflower seeds roasted and salted in our Colorful Garden Cobb Salad with Creamy Avocado Dressing (page 58).

continued

TOASTING SEEDS

You can toast seeds in three different ways: on the stovetop, in the oven, or in the microwave.

Stovetop: Place the seeds in a single layer in a heavy skillet over medium heat. Stir frequently until the seeds are warm to the touch, have begun to color lightly, and turn fragrant, 5 to 10 minutes. Watch carefully while cooking, as they can easily burn.

In the oven: Position a rack in the middle of the oven and preheat the oven to 350° F/180°C/gas 4. Spread the seeds in a single layer on an ungreased rimmed baking sheet. Bake for 5 minutes, and then stir. Bake until the seeds are warm to the touch, lightly colored, and fragrant, 5 to 10 minutes total. Watch the seeds carefully because they burn quickly.

In the microwave: Spread the seeds in a single layer on a paper towel or on a microwave-safe plate and cook on high power for 40 seconds. Depending on how hot they feel and if they have started to brown, continue to microwave in short 20-second intervals, stirring after every interval to avoid uneven cooking and burning. This method is less precise, but it's quick and convenient and gets easier with experience.

SEED MILKS

Seed milks are great nondairy substitutes for milk. The most commonly found in stores is hemp milk, but we love making homemade pumpkin seed milk, too. Simply soak 1 cup/140 g raw seeds in 3 cups/720 ml water for 8 to 12 hours in the refrigerator. After soaking, drain the seeds, discard the liquid, and rinse them. Place the seeds in the blender along with 3 cups/720 ml fresh cold water, ½ tsp pure vanilla extract, and a pinch of salt. Blend the mixture until the seeds are finely ground, and sweeten them with sugar or agave. Strain the milk through a layer of clean cheesecloth or a fine-mesh sieve. Store seed milks in a sealed container in the refrigerator for up to 4 days.

Chapter 3
SOUPS

EASY VEGETABLE STOCK

It was a challenge for me to write a recipe for vegetable stock, because in truth, mine is different every time. I am inspired to make it whenever I am prepping lots of veggies, and I realize that what I have left over—the tops of four leeks, three parsnip stubs, carrot peels and tips, and a pile of parsley stems—is almost everything I need to make a great stock. When faced with the decision to capture these flavors so they can become the foundation for future delicious soups, stews, or beans, versus adding them to my compost pile, I try to choose the former. Once you experience how much better your recipes turn out with homemade stock (not to mention how much money you save and how many cartons you keep out of the trash), you'll get more motivated. I usually keep a bag in the fridge where I save my veggie scraps, and when it gets big enough, I set my pot on the stove. The recipe below is simple and easy. You can also add corncobs, potato skins, mushroom bottoms, and even tomatoes. If you have a huge stockpot, as I do, you can easily double or triple this recipe. I keep as much stock in the refrigerator as I plan to use within 5 days and freeze the rest.   —MYRA

Makes about 2 qt/2 L

About 10 cups/1.2 kg vegetables comprising the following:

- 1 large onion (or more), cut into 1- to 2-in/2.5- to 5-cm chunks (or 3 leeks, thickly sliced)

- 2 to 4 garlic cloves, cut in half (no peeling necessary)

- 2 to 6 celery stalks (tops OK), cut into 2- to 4-in/5- to 10-cm pieces

- 2 to 4 carrots, cut into 1- to 2-in/2.5- to 5-cm pieces

- 1 bunch parsley, and more stems if available (stems are especially flavorful)

- 1 parsnip, chopped into 1- to 2-in/2.5- to 5-cm pieces (optional)

1 tsp whole black peppercorns

2 bay leaves

4 to 6 sprigs fresh thyme or 1 tsp dried thyme

In a large stockpot, combine the onion, garlic, celery, carrots, parsley, parsnip, peppercorns, bay leaves, and thyme with 4 qt/3.8 L water. Cover and bring to a boil over high heat. Reduce the heat to medium-low and simmer for 1 hour, stirring occasionally. Uncover the pot and simmer for another 20 minutes to slightly reduce the stock to intensify the flavor. Remove from the heat and let cool for at least a half hour before straining. The stock can be refrigerated, covered, for up to 1 week and frozen for up to 1 year.

1 CUP/240 ML: CALORIES: 15 | FAT: 0G | CARBS: 4G | PROTEIN: 1G | SODIUM: 60MG | VITAMIN A: 40%

RUSTIC POTATO-LEEK SOUP *with* QUICK GARLIC CROUTONS

This is a thick and satisfying soup. I call it "rustic" because the skins are left on the potatoes (they're full of fiber and vitamins) and each bite is full of chunky potatoes and fresh parsley. Our rich and crispy garlic croutons add a delectable crunch.   —MYRA

Serves 6

3 tbsp extra-virgin olive oil

3 large leeks, white part only, small dice

5 cups/1.2 L Easy Vegetable Stock (page 76) or low-sodium vegetable broth

2½ lb/1.2 kg waxy potatoes (such as Yellow Finn, German Butterball, or Ruby Crescents), medium dice

Salt

1 cup/240 ml plain, unsweetened soymilk

¼ cup/10 g packed chopped fresh flat-leaf parsley

Freshly ground black pepper

2½ cups/150 g Quick Garlic Croutons (page 57)

½ cup/15 g packed chopped fresh chives

Heat the oil in a large pot over medium heat. Add the leeks and sauté until they begin to soften, stirring frequently, for 7 to 8 minutes. Add the stock, turn the heat to high, and cook, covered, until it just begins to boil. Add the potatoes and 1 tsp salt, raise the heat to high, and cook until the stock begins to boil. Reduce the heat to low and cook at a simmer, covered, stirring occasionally, until the potatoes are soft when pierced with a fork, about 30 minutes. Add the soymilk and parsley and simmer for 3 minutes. Remove the pot from the heat and crush the potatoes with a potato masher until the stock is thickened. Season with salt and pepper.

Serve the soup topped with croutons and chives. The croutons will get soggy quickly, so serve them on the side or add them just before serving.

1 SERVING (NO TOPPINGS): CALORIES: 300 | FAT: 8G | CARBS: 49G | PROTEIN: 6G | SODIUM: 430MG | DIETARY FIBER: 20% | POTASSIUM: 29% | VITAMIN A: 35% | VITAMIN C: 70% | FOLATE: 10% | IRON: 25%

GRANDMA'S GREEN SOUP

When my kids were very young, my mom babysat almost every single day for two hours, and one of her biggest pleasures was to feed them as much healthy food as she could get them to eat. I was thrilled that my kids especially enjoyed what we all called Grandma's Green Soup—a puree of simmered vegetables that always included fresh spinach, which turned the soup green. My mom says the trick to making this soup delicious is to cook the vegetables just right—until they're tender, but not too soft. I add generous amounts of fresh parsley and dill at the very end to give it a fresh-from-the-garden flavor. Using only white and green vegetables keeps the color bright. I serve each bowl with a drizzle of good-quality olive oil and croutons, and I bring extra of both to the table since my husband likes to add more as he eats. Chives are a great alternative to croutons if you prefer. —MYRA

Serves 6 to 8

¼ cup/60 ml olive oil

3 large leeks, white part only, sliced

4 large stalks celery, sliced

1 medium parsnip, large dice

6 cups/1.4 L Easy Vegetable Stock (page 76) or low-sodium vegetable broth

2½ cups/375 g large-dice yellow potatoes

Salt

1 large cauliflower, cut into bite-size florets

1 broccoli stalk, cut into bite-size florets and medium-dice stems

2 medium zucchini, large dice

8 cups/240 g packed baby spinach

1 cup/30 g packed coarsely chopped fresh flat-leaf parsley

½ cup/15 g packed chopped fresh dill

2 tbsp fresh lemon juice

Freshly ground black pepper

Extra-virgin olive oil for drizzling

2 cups/120 g Quick Garlic Croutons (page 57)

Heat the oil in a large pot over medium heat. Add the leeks, celery, and parsnips and sauté for 6 to 8 minutes, until the vegetables begin to soften.

Add the stock, turn the heat to high, and bring the soup to the beginning of a boil. Add the potatoes and 1 tsp salt and bring to a rapid simmer. Cook, covered, for 5 minutes.

Add the cauliflower and broccoli and simmer, covered, for 5 minutes.

Add the zucchini and simmer, covered, until the potatoes are soft when pierced with a fork, about 6 to 8 minutes.

Add the spinach and simmer for 2 minutes, stirring until it's wilted. Add the parsley and dill, stir, and turn off the heat. Allow the soup to sit for a minute.

Blend the soup very thoroughly with an immersion blender right in the pot, or let it cool until it's safe to handle and blend in a food processor. Stir in the lemon juice and season with salt and pepper.

Serve the soup with a little extra-virgin olive oil drizzled over the top and croutons.

1 SERVING (NO TOPPINGS): CALORIES: 240 | FAT: 12G | CARBS: 31G | PROTEIN: 5G | SODIUM: 470MG | DIETARY FIBER: 24% | POTASSIUM: 26% | VITAMIN A: 110% | VITAMIN C: 130% | VITAMIN E: 15% | RIBOFLAVIN: 15% | VITAMIN B$_6$: 15% | FOLATE: 35% | CALCIUM: 10% | IRON: 20% | MAGNESIUM: 20%

SWEET SUMMER CORN SOUP

Perfecting this recipe required a mother-daughter collaboration. My mom started it off by cutting the kernels off the cobs, simmering the corncobs in the stock, and then scraping the cobs to capture every ounce of delicious corn flavor. Her friend Darryle Pollack taught her the trick of including potatoes and blending part of the soup to thicken it. I added warming spices like paprika and cayenne pepper to complement the sweetness of the summer corn and topped it with charred red bell peppers. Together we created a perfect soup. —MAREA

Serves 8

2 qt/2 L Easy Vegetable Stock (page 76) or low-sodium vegetable broth

6 ears fresh sweet corn

3 tbsp olive oil

2 large yellow onions, medium dice

4 large stalks celery, thinly sliced

2 tbsp fresh thyme, chopped, or 2 tsp dried thyme

1½ lb/680 g yellow potatoes (such as Yukon Gold), medium dice

Salt

½ tsp paprika

Freshly ground black pepper

Big pinch of cayenne pepper

Big pinch of ground coriander

1½ cups/360 ml plain, unsweetened soymilk

½ cup/15 g packed chopped fresh flat-leaf parsley

1 red bell pepper for garnishing

Heat the stock in a large pot until it comes to a boil, then reduce it to a simmer. While it's heating, cut off the corn kernels from the cobs (cutting in a large salad bowl helps keep the kernels from flying all over). You should have about 4½ cups/680 g of kernels. Place the 6 cobs in the stockpot, and simmer them covered, while you prepare the rest of the soup ingredients (for at least 20 minutes).

Heat the oil in a large skillet over medium heat. Sauté the onions for 3 minutes. Add the celery and thyme and sauté for another 4 minutes. Turn off the heat.

Remove the cobs from the stockpot with tongs, and place them on a plate to cool. Add the sautéed vegetables, potatoes, 1 tsp salt, paprika, ¼ tsp pepper, cayenne, and coriander to the pot and simmer, covered, for 25 minutes, stirring occasionally.

Meanwhile, when the cooked cobs are cool enough to handle, take a sturdy knife and scrape down the sides of the cobs to collect the remainder of the kernels. This should yield about 1 cup/150 g of kernel bits.

After the soup has cooked for 25 minutes, stir in the soymilk, corn kernels, and corn kernel bits. Simmer for 3 minutes. Remove 1 qt/960 ml of the soup and puree it in a blender or food processor until it's very smooth. Return the puree to the soup pot, and heat until it returns to a simmer, stirring frequently.

While the soup simmers, hold the whole bell pepper with metal tongs over an open flame on the stovetop. Turn it frequently until the skin is charred all the way around, about 5 minutes. Remove it from the heat and let cool. Using a clean dishcloth, rub off the charred skin. Remove the stem and seeds and cut the flesh into a fine dice. Set aside.

Turn off the heat for the soup and stir in the parsley. Season with salt and pepper. Ladle the soup into bowls and garnish each one with some of the red bell pepper. Serve immediately.

1 SERVING: CALORIES: 250 | FAT: 7G | CARBS: 42G | PROTEIN: 7G | SODIUM: 350MG | DIETARY FIBER: 20% | VITAMIN A: 20% | VITAMIN C: 60% | FOLATE: 15%

CURRIED YELLOW SPLIT PEA SOUP

This soup is a customer favorite at our Earthbound Farm Stand in Carmel Valley, where we make only 100 percent certified organic prepared foods. A popular destination for both locals and tourists, we're especially well known for our delicious soups that are all made with rich homemade stocks and the highest quality ingredients. We offer two hot soups every day, and one is always vegetarian. This recipe is thick, satisfying, and extremely high in protein. Just one small bowl is packed with 23 g protein.   —MYRA

Serves 6

2 tbsp canola oil

2 carrots, small dice

1 small yellow onion, medium dice

2 qt/2 L Easy Vegetable Stock (page 76) or low-sodium vegetable broth

2 cups/400 g yellow split peas

2 cups/280 g peeled medium-dice sweet potatoes

2 tsp curry powder

2 tsp ground ginger

½ tsp ground cumin

1 bay leaf

2 tbsp chopped fresh cilantro

Salt

Freshly ground black pepper

Heat the oil in a large soup pot over medium heat. Sauté the carrots and onion until the onion is translucent, about 5 minutes. Add the stock, split peas, and sweet potatoes. Bring them to a simmer and then add the curry powder, ginger, cumin, and bay leaf. Cover and simmer for 1 hour, stirring regularly.

Remove the lid and turn up the heat until the soup maintains a rapid simmer. Cook 5 to 10 minutes, stirring frequently to prevent the soup from sticking to the bottom and also to help break up the split peas. The soup is ready when it's nice and thick and the peas are soft.

Remove from the heat and stir in the cilantro; season with salt and pepper. Remove the bay leaf before serving.

1 SERVING: CALORIES: 430 | FAT: 10G | CARBS: 62G | PROTEIN: 23G | SODIUM: 870MG | DIETARY FIBER: 84% | POTASSIUM: 17% | VITAMIN A: 200% | RIBOFLAVIN: 20% | NIACIN: 30% | VITAMIN B$_6$: 20% | IRON: 15%

BUTTERNUT SQUASH SOUP *with* HAZELNUTS

This is a beautiful, nutritious, and delicious creamy soup that I make often, especially in the fall when local squash are being harvested. The addition of the sautéed tart apple gives it an especially good flavor. Our Double-Roasted Maple-Spiced Hazelnuts are a delicious topping, but if you don't have time to make them, toasted hazelnuts work just fine. The drizzle of hazelnut oil adds a nutty richness to the soup and makes it extra special.   —MYRA

Serves 4

3 tbsp extra-virgin olive oil

1 medium yellow onion, chopped

2 large garlic cloves, coarsely chopped

6 cups/780 g peeled large-dice butternut squash

1 large tart apple (such as Pippin or Granny Smith), peeled, large dice

Salt

Freshly ground black pepper

1 qt/960 ml Easy Vegetable Stock (page 76) or low-sodium vegetable broth

Toasted hazelnut oil for drizzling

½ cup/70 g Double-Roasted Maple-Spiced Hazelnuts (page 111) or hazelnuts, toasted (see page 117) and coarsely chopped

Heat 2 tbsp of the oil in a large pot on medium heat. Add the onion and sauté until it begins to soften, about 5 minutes. Add the garlic and sauté for another minute. Turn up the heat to medium-high, stir in the squash, apple, and the last 1 tbsp of the oil. Sauté until the apples just begin to soften, 8 to 10 minutes. Sprinkle with ½ tsp salt and a pinch of pepper. Stir thoroughly, then add the stock, turn the heat to high, and cover just until it begins to boil. Turn the heat to low and continue to simmer, covered, for 25 to 30 minutes, until the squash is soft when pierced with a fork.

Blend the soup with an immersion blender right in the pot, or let it cool until it's safe to handle and blend in a food processor or blender, and then return to the pot to reheat. Season with salt and pepper.

Serve the soup hot, topped with a drizzle of hazelnut oil and sprinkled with 2 tbsp of the hazelnuts.

1 SERVING (WITH PLAIN HAZELNUTS AS TOPPING, HAZELNUT OIL NOT INCLUDED): CALORIES: 400 | FAT: 22G | CARBS: 53G | PROTEIN: 8G | SODIUM: 320MG | DIETARY FIBER: 52% | POTASSIUM: 20% | VITAMIN A: 250% | VITAMIN C: 30% | VITAMIN E: 20% | THIAMIN: 20% | RIBOFLAVIN: 10% | NIACIN: 10% | VITAMIN B_6: 20% | FOLATE: 20% | CALCIUM: 10% | IRON: 15% | COPPER: 20% | PHOSPHORUS: 10% | MAGNESIUM: 15%

TOMATO-VEGETABLE SOUP *with* WHOLE-WHEAT ELBOW NOODLES

This is a simple, nourishing soup that combines a dozen delicious and healthy vegetables. It's a recipe that can easily change with the seasons, with what you have in your fridge, or what your mood inspires. If you want it to be a more filling meal, add 2 cups/500 g of cooked white beans when you add the corn. If you love potatoes, add 2 cups/240 g of cubed Yukon Golds when you add the tomatoes. In the winter you can substitute cabbage for the zucchini, and in the summer you can use fresh tomatoes instead of canned, and basil instead of parsley. If your soup turns out differently every time, it's more exciting to make again and again. I use whole-wheat elbow noodles here because my family truly prefers them to white, and they are healthier. It's best to keep the noodles separate and add them to each bowl at serving time. If the noodles are combined and stored with the soup, they will absorb the stock and get mushy. —MYRA

Serves 10

3 tbsp extra-virgin olive oil

1 large yellow onion, medium dice

2 medium carrots, sliced ⅓ in/
8 mm thick

2 medium parsnips, sliced ⅓ in/
8 mm thick

2 medium ribs celery, sliced ⅓ in/
8 mm thick

3 large garlic cloves, finely
chopped

1 tsp dried oregano

¼ tsp red pepper flakes

6 cups/1.4 L Easy Vegetable
Stock (page 76) or low-sodium
vegetable broth

One 28-oz/800-g can diced
tomatoes with juices

3 medium zucchini, sliced into
bite-size pieces

2 to 3 cups bite-size cauliflower
florets

2 cups/480 ml tomato puree or
tomato sauce

1 cup/115 g sliced string beans
(1-in/2.5-cm pieces)

Salt

Freshly ground black pepper

Put the oil in a 6-qt/5.7-L (or larger) pot over medium heat. When the oil is hot, add the onion and cook, stirring frequently, until it begins to soften, about 5 minutes. Add the carrots, parsnips, and celery and cook for 5 minutes. Add the garlic, oregano, and red pepper flakes and cook, stirring frequently, for 2 minutes.

Add the stock, cover the pot, and raise the heat to high. Bring the soup to the start of a boil, then lower the heat to maintain a slow simmer. Cook, covered, for 5 minutes, then add the tomatoes with their juices, zucchini, cauliflower, tomato puree, string beans, and ½ tsp salt, and season with pepper. Simmer the soup, covered, until the vegetables are crisp-tender, about 15 minutes. Add the spinach, corn, and parsley and cook, uncovered, for 5 minutes. Season the soup with salt and pepper.

4 cups/120 g packed baby spinach leaves, or chopped mature spinach or chard

1½ cups/210 g corn kernels, fresh or frozen

1 cup/30 g finely minced fresh flat-leaf parsley

2 cups/220 g whole-wheat elbow noodles (macaroni)

Meanwhile, cook the noodles in a large pot of salted water until al dente (be careful not to overcook). Drain the pasta and set aside while you finish the soup.

Place ⅓ cup/40 g of noodles into each bowl. Ladle in the hot soup, and stir to combine. Serve hot.

1 SERVING (WITH ⅓ CUP/40 G NOODLES): CALORIES: 240 | FAT: 5G | CARBS: 46G | PROTEIN: 8G | SODIUM: 300MG | DIETARY FIBER: 32% | POTASSIUM: 27% | VITAMIN A: 170% | VITAMIN C: 70% | VITAMIN E: 10% | THIAMIN: 20% | RIBOFLAVIN: 15% | NIACIN: 15% | VITAMIN B$_6$: 25% | FOLATE: 25% | CALCIUM: 10% | IRON: 20% | COPPER: 20% | PHOSPHORUS: 20% | MAGNESIUM: 25%

HEARTY BEET SOUP

I love beets—their earthy, sweet flavors; their bold and vivacious colors; the way they *taste* like health. This hearty soup is an homage to the incredible beet. Full of flavorful chunks of red beets and complex spices, it's unbelievably satisfying served hot and equally delicious cold. This recipe includes both the beetroot and its greens, so you don't have to waste any part of this magical vegetable. If you can't find whole bunches of beets with their greens, you can substitute the beet greens with a bunch of chard. Bursting with iron and fiber, this is the perfect soup for a boost after a long and depleting day. Even people who aren't as in love with beets as I am will enjoy this soup—as my dad will happily attest.   —MAREA

Serves 4 to 6

¼ cup/60 ml canola oil

1 large yellow onion, finely diced

3 large garlic cloves, minced

2 bay leaves

1 tbsp fennel seeds

1½ tsp ground coriander

1 tsp ground cumin

½ tsp dried thyme

Big pinch of red pepper flakes

5 cups/1.2 L Easy Vegetable Stock (page 76) or low-sodium vegetable broth

4 large beets with tops, beetroots large dice, greens finely chopped

Salt

Freshly ground black pepper

¼ cup/10 g finely chopped fresh cilantro for garnishing

Place a large pot over medium-high heat and add the oil. Stir in the onion, garlic, bay leaves, fennel seeds, coriander, cumin, thyme, and red pepper flakes and cook, stirring constantly, until the onion has softened and the mixture is fragrant, about 5 minutes. Add the stock and beets. Cover, bring to a boil, and then lower the heat to maintain a simmer. Cook, stirring occasionally, until the beets are soft and tender, 30 to 45 minutes.

Add the greens to the pot, cover, and cook for 3 minutes. Remove the soup from the heat and season with salt and pepper. Serve hot or cold, garnished with the cilantro.

1 SERVING: CALORIES: 280 | FAT: 15G | CARBS: 35G | PROTEIN: 5G | SODIUM: 540MG | DIETARY FIBER: 28% | POTASSIUM: 29% | VITAMIN A: 50% | VITAMIN C: 40% | VITAMIN E: 15% | RIBOFLAVIN: 10% | VITAMIN B$_6$: 15% | FOLATE: 45% | CALCIUM: 10% | IRON: 20% | COPPER: 15% | PHOSPHORUS: 15% | MAGNESIUM: 20%

THAI COCONUT SOUP

This soup is easy to make and bursting with flavor. Lemongrass, ginger, garlic, and jalapeño endow the stock with bold spices, and the coconut milk and lime juice added at the end transform this soup into a gentle cascade of sweetness, spice, and everything else nice. My family likes it best with a heaping tablespoon of cooked brown rice stirred in. Serve this alongside our Thai Fresh Spring Rolls with Peanut Dipping Sauce (page 99) to indulge in a delicious Thai meal without leaving the comfort of your home. —MAREA

Serves 4

1 stalk lemongrass

1 tbsp peeled minced fresh ginger

1 tbsp minced garlic

1 tbsp minced jalapeño, with or without seeds

¼ tsp red pepper flakes, plus extra as needed

2 tbsp peanut or canola oil

1 small red bell pepper, small dice

5 cups/1.2 L Easy Vegetable Stock (page 76) or low-sodium vegetable broth

2½ cups/100 g thinly sliced shiitake mushrooms

2 heads baby bok choy, thinly sliced

1 cup/160 g diced silken tofu

¾ cup/180 ml coconut milk

2 tbsp soy sauce

2 tbsp fresh lime juice

1 tsp light brown sugar

Salt

¼ cup/10 g packed chopped fresh cilantro

¼ cup/10 g packed chopped fresh basil

Cut the stem and leaf ends off the lemongrass and discard several layers of tough outer leaves. Slice the soft center of the stalk into ¼-in/6-mm pieces. Put them in a small food processor and add the ginger, garlic, jalapeño, and red pepper flakes. Process until the mixture is very fine, stopping to scrape down the sides of the bowl once or twice.

Pour the oil into a large stockpot over medium heat. Add the lemongrass-ginger mixture and the bell pepper and cook, stirring constantly, until the mixture softens and is very fragrant, 2 to 4 minutes. Add the stock, cover the pot, raise the heat to high, and bring it to a boil. Boil for 5 minutes.

Remove the cover and add the mushrooms. Reduce the heat to maintain a gentle simmer and cook, covered, until the mushrooms are soft, 5 to 8 minutes. Add the bok choy and simmer, uncovered, until it is tender, 2 to 4 minutes.

Reduce the heat to low and add the tofu, coconut milk, soy sauce, lime juice, and sugar. Stir gently to combine. Season with salt and more pepper flakes, if desired. Stir in the cilantro and basil and serve immediately.

1 SERVING: CALORIES: 300 | FAT: 18G | CARBS: 29G | PROTEIN: 10G | SODIUM: 680MG | DIETARY FIBER: 20% | POTASSIUM: 30% | VITAMIN A: 170% | VITAMIN C: 90% | VITAMIN D: 70% | VITAMIN E: 15% | THIAMIN: 10% | RIBOFLAVIN: 20% | NIACIN: 15% | VITAMIN B₆: 30% | FOLATE: 25% | CALCIUM: 20% | IRON: 30% | COPPER: 60% | PHOSPHORUS: 20% | MAGNESIUM: 20% | ZINC: 15%

SPICY CUCUMBER-GINGER GAZPACHO

This gazpacho is cool, light, and refreshing, and you never even have to turn on your stove. It's the perfect appetizer to freshen you up on a hot day, and it feels deliciously healthy to eat. Topped with fresh sweet corn and a bit of extra parsley, you'll get a mouthful of summer sunshine in every bite. —MAREA

Serves 4

2 large cucumbers, peeled and seeded if needed, coarsely chopped

1 medium yellow bell pepper, coarsely chopped

¼ cup/25 g chopped red onion

¼ cup/10 g coarsely chopped packed fresh flat-leaf parsley, plus ¼ cup/10 g finely chopped fresh flat-leaf parsley for garnishing

2 tbsp fresh lemon juice

1 tbsp finely chopped, peeled fresh ginger

1 tbsp olive oil

1 tbsp red wine vinegar

1½ tsp finely chopped seeded jalapeño

1½ tsp finely chopped garlic

¼ tsp salt

⅛ tsp freshly ground black pepper

Pinch of red pepper flakes

1 cup/140 g fresh sweet corn kernels for garnishing

Working in batches if necessary, put the cucumbers, bell pepper, onion, coarsley chopped parsley, lemon juice, ginger, oil, vinegar, jalapeño, garlic, salt, pepper, and red pepper flakes in a blender or food processor and puree until there are no large chunks left. Pour the puree into a bowl and stir in ½ cup/120 ml cold water. Refrigerate the soup for at least 30 minutes.

Garnish with the corn kernels and finely chopped parsley, and serve cold.

1 SERVING: CALORIES: 110 | FAT: 4.5G | CARBS: 18G | PROTEIN: 3G | SODIUM: 170MG | DIETARY FIBER: 16% | POTASSIUM: 14% | VITAMIN A: 45% | VITAMIN C: 60% | VITAMIN B₆: 10% | FOLATE: 10% | MAGNESIUM: 10%

Beans, Lentils, and Peas

Beans, lentils, and peas (all in the legume family) are essential to include in a plant-based diet, and we feature them in many of our favorite recipes. (Lentils, split peas, and mung beans don't require soaking, so they are fast and easy to make.) Incredibly versatile, legumes are a great source of low-fat protein, soluble and insoluble fiber, folate, potassium, iron, and magnesium (see Nutrient Chart on page 92). A common misconception is that legumes must be eaten in combination with a carbohydrate like grains or potatoes to form "complete proteins," because legumes on their own don't contain every amino acid. This has recently been disproved; as long as you are eating a varied diet that includes both legumes and other complex carbohydrates in the same 24-hour period, your body can access all the amino acids to absorb the protein available in legumes.

BEANS

Beans grow in an amazing abundance of varieties, with a vast range of flavors, colors, sizes, shapes, and uses. Buying dried beans in bulk is very economical and ecological, and freshly cooked beans taste delicious. Canned beans are extremely convenient, making it quick and easy to add them to your diet. You might find beans that are usually sold dry available fresh, like garbanzos, which are a special yummy treat roasted in their pods with olive oil and salt. Different beans contain many different nutrients, so variety is key—it's great to have so many choices to enjoy!

Presoaking Beans

Why presoak dried beans? It drastically shortens their cooking time, helps improve their digestibility, and reduces the enzymes that produce flatulence. (A good rule of thumb: The smaller the bean, the less gas it produces.) Most beans should be rinsed, then soaked for 8 hours or overnight. Beans will grow to two or three times their original size after soaking, so use a large enough pot, with enough water so that they will stay covered as they expand. After soaking, drain the beans in a colander, rinse, and then cook them in fresh water or vegetable stock (instructions follow). If you don't have time for a long soak, you can "quick-soak" them: Bring the beans and water to a boil, then turn off the heat and let the beans sit in the hot water for 1 to 2 hours. After that, they can be drained, rinsed, and cooked in the same way as soaked beans, but they may take slightly longer to cook.

How to Cook Dried Beans

Place soaked and rinsed beans back into the pot, adding water or stock until it's about 1 in/2.5 cm above the beans. Add spices such as a bay leaf, garlic, and cumin, if desired. Bring to a boil over high heat. Reduce the heat to maintain a simmer, cover, and cook for 40 minutes to 1½ hours (see Cooking Chart), until the beans are soft and can be easily smashed. If needed, add more boiling water to keep beans moist. Once the beans are ready, turn off the heat and season with salt.

COOKING CHART (for 1 cup/185 g dried beans, presoaked)

	CUPS/ML WATER	COOKING TIME
Adzuki	4 cups/960 ml	40 to 55 minutes
Black	4 cups/960 ml	1 to 1½ hours
Black-eyed peas	3 cups/720 ml	1 hour
Cannellini	3 cups/720 ml	1 to 1½ hours
Fava	3 cups/720 ml	40 to 50 minutes
Garbanzo	4 cups/960 ml	1 to 1½ hours
Great Northern	3½ cups/840 ml	1 to 1½ hours
Kidney	3 cups/720 ml	1 to 1½ hours
Lima	4 cups/960 ml	40 to 50 minutes
Navy	3 cups/720 ml	1 to 1½ hours
Pinto	3 cups/720 ml	1 to 1½ hours

continued

LENTILS

Lentils are a dietary staple for many cultures around the world. Cooked, 1 cup/200 g of lentils contains 18 g of protein and 16 g of dietary fiber. Lentils come in many varieties: brown, French green, red (which cook the fastest of all), as well as yellow, black, beluga, and pink. You can also choose whole or split lentils (we use both in our Lentil and Potato Curry, page 135). Whole lentils keep their shape, and split lentils break up easily when cooked. Lentils cook in about 30 minutes with a two-to-one water-to-lentil ratio, and should be rinsed before cooking.

SPLIT PEAS

We love cooking with split peas because they are rich, thick, and satisfying, and you can achieve amazing flavors with vegetables and spices. They are also high in protein and fiber. Split peas are available in both green and yellow, which are virtually identical except in color, although yellow peas may have a slightly milder flavor. Like lentils, they should be rinsed before cooking.

FRESH PEAS AND BEANS

Fresh green peas (English peas) are impressively rich in vitamins and minerals, including protein, vitamin K, manganese, vitamin C, and fiber. You can purchase peas fresh, frozen, or canned.

Edible-pod peas, like snow and sugar, are usually considered vegetables—their nutrition content has less protein than split peas, but they provide good sources of vitamins A, C, and fiber.

String beans, or green beans, have an impressive nutrition profile as well. Like edible-pod peas, they provide good sources of vitamins A, C, and fiber.

NUTRIENT CHART (for 1 cup/200 g cooked legumes)

	PROTEIN	FIBER	IRON	MAGNESIUM
Adzuki	17 g	17 g	4 mg	100 mg
Black	15 g	15 g	4 mg	140 mg
Black-eyed peas	15 g	12 g	5 mg	100 mg
Cannellini	15 g	11 g	5 mg	80 mg
Fava	13 g	9 g	3 mg	90 mg
Garbanzo	15 g	13 g	6 mg	100 mg
Great Northern	15 g	12 g	4 mg	120 mg
Kidney	15 g	11 g	6 mg	90 mg
Lentils	18 g	16 g	7 mg	70 mg
Lima	15 g	13 g	5 mg	90 mg
Mung	14 g	15 g	3 mg	100 mg
Navy	16 g	12 g	5 mg	110 mg
Split peas	16 g	16 g	3 mg	70 mg
Pinto	14 g	15 g	4 mg	100 mg

Chapter 4
APPETIZERS

SOBA NOODLES *with* EDAMAME, CARROTS, *and* GREEN ONIONS *in* PEANUT SAUCE

This recipe is a peanut sauce–lover's dream. Made with buckwheat soba noodles, edamame, carrots, green onions, and peanuts, this appetizer is delicious served warm or cold, and makes for ideal leftovers.   —MAREA

Serves 6

PEANUT SAUCE

½ cup/120 ml peanut butter, salted or unsalted, creamy or crunchy

½ cup very hot water (about 180°F/82°C)

1 tbsp plus 2 tsp tamari sauce

1 tbsp apple cider vinegar

1 tbsp finely chopped fresh mint

1 tbsp finely chopped fresh basil

1 tbsp agave nectar

1 tsp rice vinegar

½ tsp salt

¼ tsp garlic powder

¼ tsp ground ginger

⅛ tsp cayenne pepper

⅛ tsp pure ground chipotle chile

2 tbsp extra-virgin olive oil

10 cloves garlic, slivered

2 medium carrots, thinly sliced

1 cup/170 g shelled, cooked edamame

10 oz/280 g buckwheat soba noodles

Salt

Freshly ground black pepper

¼ cup/25 g thinly sliced green onions, white and green parts, for garnishing

½ cup/60 g roasted peanuts, chopped, for garnishing

To make the peanut sauce: Stir together the peanut butter and hot water in a small bowl until smooth. Stir in the tamari, cider vinegar, mint, basil, agave, rice vinegar, salt, garlic powder, ginger, cayenne, and chipotle until thoroughly combined. Set aside at room temperature.

Warm the oil in a large saucepan over medium heat. Add the garlic and cook, stirring constantly, for 1 minute, making sure it does not burn. Add the carrots and cook, stirring frequently, until they are crisp-tender, about 5 minutes. Remove the pan from the heat and stir in the edamame.

Bring a large pot of water to a boil over high heat and cook the soba noodles according to the package directions. Drain the noodles and add them to the saucepan with the vegetables. Add the peanut sauce and toss to combine. Season with salt and pepper. Serve warm or cold, garnished with the green onions and peanuts.

1 SERVING: CALORIES: 360 | FAT: 23G | CARBS: 30G | PROTEIN: 15G | SODIUM: 530MG | DIETARY FIBER: 20% | VITAMIN A: 180% | VITAMIN E: 15% | NIACIN: 20% | VITAMIN B$_6$: 20% | PHOSPHORUS: 15% | MAGNESIUM: 20%

THAI FRESH SPRING ROLLS *with* PEANUT DIPPING SAUCE

Making Thai spring rolls is one of my favorite kitchen activities—it's especially fun to wrap them with a group of friends when we want to get creative with our food. They look impressive but are surprisingly easy to make. The tofu needs to be marinated and baked, but the other ingredients require minimal prep time. They taste best eaten right away, but if you cover them with a damp paper towel and refrigerate, they can be stored for up to 24 hours. Served alongside our delicious peanut sauce, this is always a popular appetizer—as good as any spring rolls you will eat in a restaurant.   —MAREA

Serves 6; makes 12 rolls

PEANUT SAUCE

¼ cup/60 ml peanut butter, salted or unsalted, creamy or crunchy

¼ cup/60 ml very hot water (about 180°F/82°C)

1 tbsp soy sauce

1 tbsp rice vinegar

2 tsp agave nectar

1 tsp fresh lime juice

⅛ tsp salt

Freshly ground black pepper

TOFU

1 tbsp low-sodium soy sauce

1 tbsp extra-virgin olive oil

⅛ tsp freshly ground black pepper

8 oz/225 g extra-firm tofu, cut into twelve 3-by-½-in/7.5-cm-by-12-mm sticks

SPRING ROLLS

1 cup/170 g cooked rice noodles, prepared according to package directions

12 cucumber sticks, 3 by ¼ in/7.5 cm by 6 mm

12 carrot sticks, 3 by ¼ in/7.5 cm by 6 mm

To make the peanut sauce: Stir together the peanut butter and hot water in a small bowl until smooth. Add the soy sauce, vinegar, agave, lime juice, salt, and a pinch of pepper and stir until thoroughly combined. Set aside at room temperature.

To make the tofu: Position a rack in the middle of the oven and preheat it to 375°F/190°C/gas 5. Whisk together the soy sauce, oil, and pepper in a small bowl. Drain the tofu sticks on paper towels to remove excess water. Place the tofu on a small rimmed baking sheet or in a casserole dish and pour the marinade evenly over each piece. Make sure every side is thoroughly coated. Allow the tofu to marinate for at least 10 to 15 minutes before baking.

Bake the tofu on the middle rack for 15 minutes. Remove it from the oven, flip each stick over, then bake for another 15 minutes, or until golden brown.

To make the spring rolls: Place the noodles, cucumber, carrot, bean sprouts, avocado, lettuce, mint, cilantro, and tofu on individual plates around your work surface.

Fill a wide, shallow bowl with warm water. Place one spring roll wrapper in the bowl and let it soak until limp, about 5 seconds. Lay the wrapper down flat on your work surface. In the upper center section of the wrapper, place 1 piece of lettuce. You will want to leave at least 1 in/2.5 cm at the bottom of the wrapper uncovered; no need to leave any space at the top. In a compact vertical line, arrange 1 piece each of carrot, cucumber, tofu, and avocado, a generous 1 tbsp each of the bean sprouts and noodles, and 1 tsp each of the mint and cilantro.

continued

1 cup/85 g packed mung bean sprouts

1 ripe avocado, sliced lengthwise into 12 even pieces

12 pieces heirloom or romaine lettuce, torn into 3-by-3-in/ 7.5-by-7.5-cm pieces

¼ cup/10 g coarsely chopped fresh spearmint

¼ cup/10 g fresh cilantro

Twelve 6-in/15-cm spring roll wrappers

Fold the bottom edge of the wrapper on top of the filling. Then tightly (but gently) pull the left edge of the wrapper over the filling and the folded bottom edge. It may be helpful to put pressure on the filling with your fingertips to make it as compact as possible while rolling. Pull and roll the left side over the right side of the wrapper, keeping the filling as compact as possible. Press the edges of the wrapper together to close. You will have the top of the spring roll open, and tightly wrapped bottom and sides. Repeat until all 12 spring rolls are assembled. Serve with the peanut sauce.

2 ROLLS (WITH 1 TBSP PEANUT SAUCE): CALORIES: 340 | FAT: 18G | CARBS: 33G | PROTEIN: 16G | SODIUM: 290MG | DIETARY FIBER: 20% | VITAMIN A: 60% | VITAMIN C: 20% | THIAMIN: 10% | FOLATE: 25% | CALCIUM: 15% | IRON: 15% | COPPER: 20% | PHOSPHORUS: 20% | MAGNESIUM: 20%

SHIITAKE MUSHROOM, WATER CHESTNUT, *and* TOFU LETTUCE CUPS

My son says this vegan version of Chinese-style lettuce wraps may be his favorite recipe in this cookbook. Shiitakes add great health benefits and flavor, and I use a generous amount of water chestnuts, because I love their crunch. If you prep everything beforehand, this appetizer will be ready in just 15 minutes. Lettuce wraps are fun to eat, too. Simply place a spoonful of the stir-fry in a lettuce leaf, fold it up, and take a bite. This is the only dish I ever make at home that features iceberg lettuce. It's crisp and succulent—perfect for these wraps. Romaine lettuce also works.   —MYRA

Serves 4

2 tbsp peanut oil

6 oz/170 g firm tofu, small dice

5 oz/140 g canned water chestnuts, small dice

1 tbsp soy sauce

4 cups/160 g small-dice shiitake mushrooms

2 tbsp very hot water (about 180°F/82°C)

STIR-FRY SAUCE

2 tbsp toasted sesame oil

1 tbsp plus 2 tsp soy sauce

3 large garlic cloves, crushed

1 tbsp peeled, finely grated fresh ginger

1½ tsp unseasoned rice vinegar

1 tsp brown sugar

⅛ tsp red pepper flakes

½ cup/45 g sliced green onions, white bulb plus 2 in/5 cm of green

1 large head iceberg lettuce

Heat 1 tbsp of the peanut oil in a 12-in/30.5-cm nonstick skillet (preferably cast iron) over medium-high heat. Add the tofu and cook, stirring occasionally, until it is golden, about 5 minutes. Add the water chestnuts and cook for 1 minute. Add the soy sauce and cook, stirring often, for 2 minutes. Transfer the mixture to a bowl and set aside.

Reduce the heat to medium and add the remaining 1 tbsp of the peanut oil to the skillet. Add the mushrooms and hot water and stir. Cover and cook for 5 minutes, stirring occasionally.

Meanwhile, make the stir-fry sauce: Whisk together the sesame oil, soy sauce, garlic, ginger, vinegar, sugar, and red pepper flakes in a small bowl.

Add the tofu–water chestnut mixture, green onions, and stir-fry sauce to the skillet with the mushrooms. Cook, stirring continually, until the sauce is absorbed, 2 to 3 minutes.

Meanwhile, core the lettuce and discard the outer leaves. Separate the remaining leaves; rinse and dry them and lay them on a large plate.

Transfer the stir-fry either to one serving bowl or divide it among four small bowls. Serve it with the lettuce leaves.

1 SERVING: CALORIES: 260 | FAT: 17G | CARBS: 23G | PROTEIN: 9G | SODIUM: 780MG | DIETARY FIBER: 20% | POTASSIUM: 15% | VITAMIN A: 20% | VITAMIN C: 15% | VITAMIN D: 45% | RIBOFLAVIN: 10% | VITAMIN B₆: 15% | FOLATE: 20% | CALCIUM: 15% | IRON: 15% | COPPER: 35% | PHOSPHORUS: 15% | MAGNESIUM: 15% | ZINC: 10%

STUFFED MUSHROOMS *with* ARUGULA, WALNUTS, *and* SUN-DRIED TOMATOES

These mushrooms are stuffed with a delicious mixture of peppery arugula, sweet sun-dried tomatoes, and crunchy toasted walnuts. Flavored with balsamic vinegar and topped with a sprinkling of fresh chopped parsley, this unique appetizer can be served warm out of the oven or at room temperature. You can make the stuffing up to 3 days in advance. Before serving, just fill the mushrooms and pop them in the oven so they—and you—are ready for the party.   —MAREA

Serves 6

3 tbsp olive oil

⅓ cup/35 g finely diced red onion

2 tbsp finely chopped garlic

4 cups/120 g finely chopped packed baby spinach

½ cup/55 g finely chopped walnuts, toasted (see page 117)

⅓ cup/60 g oil-packed sun-dried tomatoes, drained and finely chopped

2 cups/100 g finely chopped packed arugula

⅓ cup plus 2 tbsp/15 g packed finely chopped fresh flat-leaf parsley

½ cup/40 g panko bread crumbs

1 tbsp plus 1 tsp balsamic vinegar

½ tsp salt

¼ tsp freshly ground black pepper

1½ lb/680 g cremini mushrooms, 2 to 2½ in/5 to 6 cm in diameter, stemmed

1 tbsp plus 2 tsp raw pine nuts

Position a rack in the middle of the oven and preheat it to 375°F/ 190°C/gas 5. Lightly oil a rimmed baking sheet and set aside.

Warm the oil in a medium skillet over medium heat. Add the onion and garlic and cook, stirring frequently, until the mixture softens and turns fragrant, about 5 minutes.

Reduce the heat to medium-low and add the spinach, walnuts, and tomatoes. Sauté for another 2 minutes, or until the spinach wilts.

Add the arugula, ⅓ cup/20 g of the parsley, and the panko, and stir to combine. Turn off the heat. Add the vinegar, salt, and pepper.

To stuff the mushrooms, place them on the prepared baking sheet, tops down. Fill each mushroom cavity with about 1 tbsp of the filling, or however much they can hold. Place a few pine nuts on top of each mushroom.

Bake the mushrooms for 20 to 25 minutes, or until they are tender when pierced with a knife. Remove the baking sheet from the oven and let the mushrooms cool for 5 minutes. Garnish with the remaining 2 tbsp of the parsley and let cool for at least 3 minutes. Serve immediately or at room temperature.

1 SERVING: CALORIES: 250 | FAT: 16G | CARBS: 23G | PROTEIN: 10G | SODIUM: 420MG | DIETARY FIBER: 32% | POTASSIUM: 35% | VITAMIN A: 260% | VITAMIN C: 35% | VITAMIN E: 15% | THIAMIN: 20% | RIBOFLAVIN: 40% | NIACIN: 35% | VITAMIN B₆: 25% | FOLATE: 60% | CALCIUM: 25% | IRON: 50% | COPPER: 50% | PHOSPHORUS: 25% | MAGNESIUM: 40% | ZINC: 15%

CROSTINI *with* VINE-RIPE TOMATOES *and* WHITE BEAN PUREE

This appetizer is a toast to the tomato—ideal for summer and early fall when vine-ripe tomatoes are at their peak. Heirloom varieties, like rich-flavored, deep red Brandywines, make these crostini all the more memorable. The avocado is optional, but it contributes another layer of flavor and texture. I add them when my tomatoes are just so-so, or if I have a ripe one on my counter begging to be used. While basil might be a more traditional partner to tomatoes, I find the Italian parsley perfectly complements both the tomatoes and the white bean puree. —MYRA

Serves 4

WHITE BEAN PUREE

1½ cups/255 ml cooked white beans (drained and rinsed if canned)

¼ cup/60 ml extra-virgin olive oil

2 tbsp golden balsamic vinegar

2 tsp coarsely chopped garlic

¾ tsp salt

⅛ tsp white pepper

CROSTINI

1 cup/30 g chopped fresh flat-leaf parsley

2 tbsp extra-virgin olive oil

1 tbsp plus 1 tsp coarsely chopped garlic

Salt

Freshly ground black pepper

Eight ½- to ¾-in-/12- to 20-mm-thick baguette slices, preferably whole wheat or multigrain, toasted

1 ripe avocado, thinly sliced into at least 16 pieces (optional)

Eight ⅓-in-/8-mm-thick vine-ripe tomato slices, heirlooms preferred

To make the bean puree: Combine the beans, oil, vinegar, garlic, salt, and white pepper in a food processor and process until smooth. Set aside at room temperature.

To make the crostini: In a small bowl, mix together the parsley, oil, garlic, ½ tsp salt, and a pinch of black pepper.

Spread each slice of toasted baguette with approximately 2 tbsp of the bean puree. Top each with 1½ tsp of the parsley mixture, 2 slices of avocado (if using), and then 1 slice of tomato. Top the tomato with 1½ tsp more of the parsley mixture and season with salt and pepper. Serve immediately.

2 CROSTINI (WITHOUT AVOCADO): CALORIES: 400 | FAT: 19G | CARBS: 47G | PROTEIN: 15G | SODIUM: 970MG | DIETARY FIBER: 40% | POTASSIUM: 25% | VITAMIN A: 40% | VITAMIN C: 50% | THIAMIN: 20% | RIBOFLAVIN: 10% | NIACIN: 15% | VITAMIN B_6: 15% | FOLATE: 30% | CALCIUM: 15% | IRON: 30% | COPPER: 30% | PHOSPHORUS: 25% | MAGNESIUM: 25% | ZINC: 15%

FRIED GREEN TOMATOES

Fried green tomatoes are a popular and ubiquitous dish in the South but a novelty to many people from other regions of the country. This is a tasty way to use tomatoes from your garden that haven't yet ripened; green tomatoes are also sold at many farmers' markets starting in midsummer. Our version results in a tart, meltingly soft slice of tomato enclosed in a crunchy crust of flour, panko bread crumbs, and cornmeal—a yummy, rich indulgence. Two or three tomato slices are a perfect serving size. And be careful not to burn your mouth—these fried green tomatoes get astonishingly hot. —MYRA

Serves 6; makes 12 to 16 slices

¾ cup/180 ml plain, unsweetened soymilk

2 tbsp fresh lemon juice

1 tbsp extra-virgin olive oil

½ cup/70 g whole-wheat pastry flour

2½ tsp salt

¼ tsp cayenne pepper

Pinch of sweet paprika

1 cup/80 g panko bread crumbs

1 cup/150 g cornmeal

High-heat oil for frying, such as safflower

4 large green tomatoes (about 3½ in/9 cm in diameter), cut into ⅓-in/8-mm-thick slices

In a shallow bowl, whisk together the soymilk and lemon juice and let sit for 5 minutes until it thickens into "buttermilk." Beat in the olive oil.

In another shallow bowl or rimmed plate, whisk the flour with 1½ tsp of the salt, the cayenne, and paprika.

In another shallow bowl or rimmed plate, combine the bread crumbs, cornmeal, and the remaining 1 tsp salt.

Heat about 3 tbsp of the frying oil in a skillet (preferably cast iron) over medium heat. If you have two skillets, use them both so that you can cook all the tomatoes at once.

To prepare the tomato slices, first dredge each in the flour mixture, then into the "buttermilk," and then coat with the cornmeal mixture. Ready a plate lined with several layers of paper towels. Transfer the tomatoes to the hot skillet, making sure they don't touch. Cook until they are golden brown on one side, about 6 minutes. Using a spatula, flip the tomatoes over and cook until the second side is golden brown and the tomatoes are tender, about 5 minutes. Transfer the tomatoes to the paper towel–lined plate to absorb any excess oil. Serve hot.

1 **SERVING:** CALORIES: 300 | FAT: 16G | CARBS: 36G | PROTEIN: 7G | SODIUM: 1040MG | DIETARY FIBER: 24% |
POTASSIUM: 15% | VITAMIN A: 25% | VITAMIN C: 70% | VITAMIN E: 15% | THIAMIN: 15% | NIACIN: 15% |
VITAMIN B$_6$: 15% | IRON: 15% | COPPER: 15% | PHOSPHORUS: 15% | MAGNESIUM: 15%

THREE-COLOR HUMMUS *with* GARLIC–WHOLE WHEAT PITA CHIPS

This recipe is my standby for virtually any gathering or potluck. And it's a standout, thanks to the varied flavors and three colors: classic beige, sun-dried tomato red, and spinach and herb green. I usually serve this hummus selection with assorted olives and cut-up veggies. My favorites are peppers, carrots, celery, radishes, cucumbers, and jicama. Homemade pita chips are another great accompaniment—tastier as well as healthier than store-bought versions. While I often cook my own beans, canned are very convenient, and they work perfectly fine for hummus.   —MYRA

Serves 8 to 12

4½ cups/720 g cooked garbanzo beans (rinsed and drained if canned)

⅔ cup/165 ml tahini

⅓ cup plus 2 tbsp/105 ml extra-virgin olive oil

⅓ cup plus 1 tbsp/90 ml fresh lemon juice

3 large garlic cloves, coarsely chopped

2 tsp salt

Freshly ground black pepper

¼ cup plus 1 tsp/50 g oil-packed sun-dried tomatoes, drained and chopped

1¼ cups/40 g packed baby spinach

½ cup/15 g packed fresh flat-leaf parsley

Garlic–Whole Wheat Pita Chips (page 108)

Fit a food processor with the steel blade. Combine the beans, tahini, ⅓ cup/75 ml of the oil, ⅓ cup/75 ml of the lemon juice, the garlic, ½ cup/120 ml water, 2 tsp salt, and a few grinds of pepper in the food processor. Process until the mixture is smooth, stopping at least once to scrape down the sides of the bowl. If the hummus is thicker than desired, thin it by adding 2 tbsp at a time of cold water. Remove 1⅔ cups/360 g of the puree and transfer it to a serving bowl. Season with salt and pepper. This is the classic hummus.

Remove an additional 1⅔ cups/360 g of the hummus and set aside (this will become the green hummus).

Red Hummus: Add the sun-dried tomatoes and 2 tbsp water to the hummus remaining in the food processor. Process until the mixture is smooth. Season with salt and pepper. Transfer the red hummus to a serving bowl.

Green Hummus: Rinse the food processor bowl and blade. Place the spinach and parsley in the bowl and pulse until the mixture is finely chopped. Add the reserved plain hummus, and the remaining 2 tbsp oil and 1 tbsp lemon juice. Process until smooth, and season with salt and pepper. Transfer the green hummus to a serving bowl.

Serve with pita chips.

2 TSP/28 G CLASSIC HUMMUS: CALORIES: 70 | FAT: 4G | CARBS: 6G | PROTEIN: 2G | SODIUM: 115MG

2 TSP/28 G RED HUMMUS: CALORIES: 70 | FAT: 4G | CARBS: 6G | PROTEIN: 2G | SODIUM: 110MG

2 TSP/28 G GREEN HUMMUS: CALORIES: 70 | FAT: 4G | CARBS: 5G | PROTEIN: 2G | SODIUM: 100MG

GARLIC–WHOLE WHEAT PITA CHIPS

Serves 8

¼ cup/60 ml extra-virgin olive oil

2 tbsp pressed garlic

¼ tsp salt

4 whole-wheat pitas, split in half

Position a rack in the lower third of the oven and preheat it to 350°F/ 180°C/gas 4.

Whisk together the oil, garlic, and salt. With a pastry brush, brush the split side surfaces of the pita bread with the oil and garlic mixture. Cut each pita round in half, and then cut each half into 3 or 4 pie-shaped wedges. Arrange the chips in a single layer on a rimmed baking sheet. You may need two baking sheets. Bake for 10 minutes, or until the pitas are fragrant and they begin to crisp. Remove the tray from the oven and let the chips cool before serving. Please note that these chips will get soggy after a few hours, especially when the weather is humid.

1 SERVING: CALORIES: 150 | FAT: 8G | CARBS: 18G | PROTEIN: 3G | SODIUM: 240MG | DIETARY FIBER: 8%

CRISPY BAKED KALE CHIPS

Kale chips are my favorite snack. I love the satisfying crunch of this healthy green when baked, the exciting combination of spices, and the cheesy flavor of the nutritional yeast (see Note, page 61). It's the perfect food to eat while lounging and watching a movie or as a quick midday snack. Feel free to experiment with many different spices. Get creative with it, and relish the fact that your snack food is made from one of the healthiest vegetables on earth!   —MAREA

Serves 4

1 tbsp plus 1 tsp extra-virgin olive oil

1 tsp fresh lemon juice

½ tsp curry powder

½ tsp salt

⅛ tsp cayenne pepper

⅛ tsp freshly ground black pepper

8 oz/225 g destemmed dino (Tuscan) or curly kale, cut into 2 in/5-cm strips

¼ cup/20 g nutritional yeast

Position a rack in the middle of the oven and preheat it to 300°F/150°C/gas 2.

In a small bowl, whisk together the oil, lemon juice, curry powder, salt, cayenne, and pepper.

Put the kale in a very large mixing bowl, making sure it is completely dry (excess water will make the chips soggy). Massage the oil mixture into the kale, making sure that each leaf is coated equally. Then sprinkle it with the yeast and mix thoroughly with your hands until each piece is evenly coated.

Arrange the kale in a single layer on two large baking sheets, and place them in the oven on the middle racks. Bake for about 40 minutes, until the kale is crispy. Serve warm or at room temperature.

1 SERVING. CALORIES: 60 | FAT: 4G | CARBS: 5G | PROTEIN: 3G | SODIUM: 300MG | VITAMIN A: 150% | VITAMIN C: 40%

DOUBLE-ROASTED MAPLE-SPICED HAZELNUTS

These sweet-savory nuts are nutritious snacks that are almost addictive. Tossed in a combination of pure maple syrup, cayenne, and salt, the nuts take on a light glaze when roasted (pictured on the facing page, middle). Unless you can find blanched hazelnuts, you'll need to roast the nuts twice; once to remove the skins, and a second time to create the coating. We like these nuts as a garnish for our Butternut Squash Soup (page 83), as well as a topping for Cress, Belgian Endive, Persimmon, and Hazelnut Salad (page 53). If you make a large batch, you can use them as a hostess or holiday gift, as long as you can resist eating them all yourself. —MYRA

Makes 1 cup/140 g

1 cup/140 g raw hazelnuts

1½ tbsp pure maple syrup

⅛ tsp cayenne pepper

⅛ tsp salt

Position a rack in the upper third of the oven and preheat it to 350°F/180°C/gas 4.

Spread the nuts on a rimmed baking sheet and bake for 10 to 15 minutes, or until the skins begin to loosen and crack. Remove from the oven and allow them to cool for about 10 minutes. Transfer the nuts to a clean kitchen towel and rub vigorously to remove the loose skins. (Little bits of skin will remain on some nuts; this is normal and extra baking time won't help).

Line the rimmed baking sheet with a piece of parchment paper and set aside.

Place the skinned hazelnuts in a small bowl and add the syrup. Toss to coat, then add the cayenne and salt, tossing again.

Transfer the nuts to the prepared baking sheet, spreading them in a single layer so that they do not touch. Bake for 10 to 15 minutes, until the nuts are glazed and fragrant. Cool completely before transferring them to an airtight container. The nuts will keep, tightly covered, at room temperature for up to 3 weeks.

¼ CUP/30 G: CALORIES: 200 | FAT: 17G | CARBS: 10G | PROTEIN: 4G | SODIUM: 75MG | DIETARY FIBER: 12% | VITAMIN E: 20% | THIAMIN: 10% | COPPER: 25% | MAGNESIUM: 10%

COCONUT-CURRY CASHEWS

These unusual nuts are perfect to put out for guests, bring as a hostess gift in a recycled tin, or just nibble on when you want a healthy snack (pictured in the photo on page 110, bottom). Raw cashews are coated with coconut milk and curry and partially roasted, then more coconut milk and a sprinkling of shredded coconut are added before the roasting is complete. Delicate coconut burns quickly, so keep a close eye on the nuts during the final minutes of cooking. Cool completely before you store them in an airtight container. They are best consumed within a week.   —MYRA

Makes 1½ cups/210 g

1½ cups/210 g raw unsalted cashews

3 tbsp coconut milk

2 tsp agave nectar

1½ tsp curry powder

1 tsp soy sauce

Pinch of ground coriander

Pinch of salt

2 tbsp shredded unsweetened coconut

Set a rack in the middle of the oven and preheat it to 325°F/165°C/gas 3. Cover a baking sheet with parchment paper.

In a medium bowl, using your hands or two large spoons, thoroughly combine the cashews with 2 tbsp of the coconut milk, 1 tsp of the agave, the curry powder, soy sauce, coriander, and salt. Spread the nuts out evenly on the baking sheet and bake for 5 minutes. Stir the nuts and then return them to the oven for an additional 5 minutes.

Remove the nuts from the oven and, with a spatula or wooden spoon, scoop the nuts into a mound in the middle of the baking pan. Drizzle them with the remaining 1 tbsp of the coconut milk and 1 tsp agave and toss the nuts using two large spoons or two spatulas (or one of each). Sprinkle the coconut over the nuts, and toss again. Spread the nuts out evenly on the baking sheet and bake for 5 more minutes. They will be lightly golden brown when done. If they are not ready after 5 minutes, return them to the oven, stirring every minute or two, keeping a close eye out not to burn the nuts or the coconut.

Allow the nuts to cool completely before serving. Store cooled nuts in an airtight container for up to 1 week.

¼ CUP/35 G: CALORIES: 230 | FAT: 18G | CARBS: 13G | PROTEIN: 7G | SODIUM: 160MG | IRON: 15% | COPPER: 40% | PHOSPHORUS: 20% | MAGNESIUM: 25% | ZINC: 15%

CHIPOTLE-LIME BRAZIL NUTS

These toasted Brazil nuts are smoky and sweet, tangy and spicy (pictured in the photo on page 110, top). Brazil nuts are known for being the best source in the world for selenium, a trace mineral essential to good health. This recipe is simple and very easy to make, and perfect to serve as an appetizer along with our Double-Roasted Maple-Spiced Hazelnuts (page 111) and Coconut-Curry Cashews (facing page). Let them cool completely before you store them in an airtight container. They are best consumed within a week.   —MAREA

Makes 2 cups/260 g

2 cups/260 g raw unsalted Brazil nuts, cut in half widthwise

1 tbsp fresh lime juice

2½ tsp maple syrup

1 tsp olive oil

¾ tsp pure ground chipotle chile

¼ tsp salt

Set a rack in the middle of the oven and preheat it to 325°F/165°C/gas 3. Cover a baking sheet with parchment paper.

In a medium bowl, using your hands or two large spoons, thoroughly mix the Brazil nuts, lime juice, maple syrup, olive oil, chipotle, and salt together.

Spread the nuts out evenly on the baking sheet and bake for 5 minutes. Remove and stir and then return them to the oven for an additional 10 to 15 minutes, until the nuts are golden brown.

Allow the nuts to cool completely before serving. Store cooled nuts in an airtight container for up to 1 week.

¼ CUP/40 G: CALORIES: 240 | FAT: 24G | CARBS: 6G | PROTEIN: 5G | SODIUM: 75MG | THIAMIN: 15% | COPPER: 30% | PHOSPHORUS: 25% | MAGNESIUM: 35%

CAMILLE *and* MAREA'S FAVORITE POPCORN

My best friend, Camille, and I love making popcorn together. To be honest, she's really the expert—I'm usually her sous-chef and eating partner. This popcorn recipe is our absolute favorite. With savory spices, lemon juice, and nutritional yeast added at the end, this version will expand your concept of what popcorn can be. We love eating it with fresh baby spinach leaves—although it sounds like a strange combination, spinach really does complement the popcorn perfectly. I can't think of a much better "snack and chat" appetizer than this recipe served with Fresh Mint and Cilantro Ice Tea (facing page). It's important to make this recipe right before serving. The moisture from the lemon and spinach makes it get soggy more quickly than traditional popcorn.   —MAREA

Serves 4

½ cup/110 g popcorn kernels

3 tbsp/60 ml olive oil

1 tsp dried oregano

¾ tsp garlic powder

¼ tsp sweet paprika

⅛ tsp red pepper flakes

2 tbsp fresh lemon or lime juice

2 tbsp nutritional yeast (see Note, page 61)

1 tsp salt

¼ tsp freshly ground black pepper

4 cups/120 g packed baby spinach leaves (optional)

Put the popcorn and oil in a large thick-bottomed pot over medium heat. Stir to combine. Cover the pot, leaving the lid slightly ajar so that the steam can escape.

The popcorn will start to pop in about 4 to 5 minutes. There is no need to shake the pot (but if you want to, go ahead). Once the popping slows, remove the pot from the heat until the popping stops completely, and transfer the popcorn to a large bowl.

While the popcorn pops, toast the spices by combining the oregano, garlic powder, paprika, and red pepper flakes in a small dry pan. Cook over medium heat, stirring almost continuously, for about 4 minutes, until the spices are toasted and aromatic.

Drizzle the popcorn with the lemon juice and sprinkle it with the yeast, salt, pepper, and toasted spices. Stir with your hands or two large mixing spoons to make sure the popcorn is thoroughly coated.

Add the spinach, if using, and serve immediately.

1 SERVING (WITH SPINACH): CALORIES: 210 | FAT: 12G | CARBS: 23G | PROTEIN: 5G | SODIUM: 600MG | DIETARY FIBER: 20% | VITAMIN A: 40% | VITAMIN C: 15% | IRON: 10%

1 SERVING (NO SPINACH): CALORIES: 200 | FAT: 12G | CARBS: 22G | PROTEIN: 4G | SODIUM: 580MG | DIETARY FIBER: 16%

Fresh Mint and Cilantro Ice Tea

I discovered that mint and cilantro complement each other perfectly when I was at a ten-day silent meditation retreat in Chile—but alas, I couldn't tell anybody about it! Every day, I would make myself tea with whatever herbs were available, experimenting with all different flavors, until I came upon this magic duo. Simultaneously tantalizing and refreshing, this ice tea is the perfect cold drink to enjoy on a warm day when all you want to do is sit and smile.   —MAREA

Serves 4

3 cups/720 ml very hot water
(about 180°F/82°C)

5 oz/140 g fresh mint

3 oz/85 g fresh cilantro

Submerge the mint and cilantro leaves in the hot water. Let sit at room temperature for about 1 hour, and then refrigerate until cold, about 1½ to 2 hours.

Place 2 cups/480 ml ice cubes in a large serving glass. Pour the tea over a mesh strainer into the glass, discarding the leaves. Serve cold.

Nuts

Nuts form an important part of a plant-based diet. Packed full of key nutrients like protein, healthy fats, antioxidants, vitamins, and minerals, they provide long-lasting energy that helps maintain healthy blood sugar levels and keep us satisfied for longer periods of time. Nature's perfect snack food, nuts are ideal for quick and easy nutrition on the go. Nuts contribute fabulous flavors, textures, and crunch to every type of recipe in this book.

ALMONDS

Almonds have it all. Not only are they tasty but they're also, ounce for ounce, one of the most nutritious nuts on earth, with 6 g protein per 1 oz/30 g serving, plus 35 percent of your daily value for vitamin E. Almonds are available in a huge variety of forms, including flour, paste, milk, and oil, as well as raw, roasted, slivered, and sliced.

CASHEWS

With their soft texture and buttery flavor, crescent-shaped cashews are perfect snacks and versatile enough to use in sauces and dressings. Cashews are a good source of protein, with 5 g per 1 oz/30 g.

HAZELNUTS

Also called filberts, hazelnuts have a unique and wonderful flavor. We like them as toppings for salads, soups, and cereals and also in baked goods. Hazelnuts have a high vitamin E content compared to other nuts, providing 45 percent of your daily value, as well as 4 g protein in each 1 oz/30 g serving.

PEANUTS

Peanuts are actually legumes—but they function exactly like other nuts and make a wonderful, satisfying snack, with a whopping 7 g protein per 1 oz/30 g serving. Sweet or savory, toasted or ground into peanut butter, the humble peanut is full of creative potential.

PECANS

Soft, sweet pecans crisp up wonderfully when toasted. We use them in our breakfasts and desserts and appreciate their delicious flavor and crunch on salads. Pecans have 3 g protein per 1 oz/30 gram serving, as well as 11 percent of your daily value for fiber.

PINE NUTS

Inside pinecones are small edible pine nuts, also called pinoli, piñons, or pignoli nuts. Their rich, sweet taste adds a delectable flavor and texture to many types of dishes, both sweet and savory. They have 4 g protein per 1 oz/30g.

PISTACHIOS

Pistachios have a delicious, buttery flavor and a gorgeous green color that distinguishes them from other nuts. You can find shelled or unshelled pistachios in stores, as well as roasted, raw, salted, and unsalted. Each 1 oz/30 g serving of pistachios contains 6 g protein.

WALNUTS

With a higher amount of omega-3 fatty acids than any other nuts, as well as 50 percent of your daily value of manganese and 4 g protein per 1 oz/30 g, walnuts are a delicious and versatile power food.

MACADAMIAS

Macadamia nuts, native to Australia, have a buttery taste and creamy texture. They are low in protein compared to other nuts (with 1 g in every 1 oz/30 g serving) but very high in manganese, containing 45 percent of your daily value.

BRAZILS

Brazil nuts, native to South America, are extremely flavorful. Each 1 oz/30 g contains 4 g protein, 26 percent of your daily value of magnesium, 24 percent of copper, and an exceptionally high level of selenium: a whopping 767 percent of your daily value!

TOASTING NUTS

Properly toasting nuts releases their essential oils, making them more fragrant, flavorful, and crunchy. Whichever method you choose, toast them until they are fragrant and golden brown. Watch carefully while cooking; they can easily burn. When recipes call for "lightly toasted" nuts, toast until they just begin to color slightly. Cooking times will vary. In general, the smaller the nuts, the faster they will cook. Nuts get crunchy as they cool, and toasting shortens their shelf life. Store them in an airtight container in a cool, dry location for up to 2 weeks.

continued

Stovetop: Place the nuts in a single layer in a heavy skillet (preferably cast iron) over medium heat. Stir frequently until the nuts are warm to the touch, have begun to color lightly, and turn fragrant, 5 to 10 minutes.

In the oven: Position a rack in the middle of the oven and preheat the oven to 350°F/180°C/gas 4. Spread the nuts in a single layer on an ungreased rimmed baking sheet. Bake for 5 minutes, and then stir. Cook until the nuts are warm to the touch, lightly colored, and fragrant, 5 to 15 minutes.

In the microwave: Cooking times will vary by the amount of nuts being toasted. Smaller quantities will toast much faster than larger quantities. Spread the nuts in a single layer on a paper towel or on a microwave-safe plate and cook on high power for 40 seconds. Depending on how hot they feel and if they have started to brown, continue to microwave in 10- to 20-second intervals, stirring after every interval. This method is less precise, but it's quick and convenient and gets easier with experience.

NUT MILKS

Nut milks are a delicious and healthy alternative to dairy. To create your own, soak about 1 cup/140 g of raw, unsalted nuts in 3 cups/720 ml water for 8 to 12 hours in the refrigerator. After soaking, drain and discard the liquid, and rinse the nuts. Place the nuts in a blender, and add 3 cups/960 ml of cold water, ½ tsp of pure vanilla extract, and a pinch of salt. Blend the mixture until the nuts are finely ground, and then strain the milk through a layer of clean cheesecloth or a fine-mesh sieve. If desired, sweeten to taste with sugar, agave, or maple syrup. Store nut milks in a sealed container in the refrigerator for up to 4 days.

Almond and hazelnut milks are the most common varieties found in stores, but you can use these directions to make nut milks with Brazil nuts, macadamia nuts, pecans, or walnuts. You can also experiment with combining two or three types of nuts for unique blends. Cashews, pine nuts, and pistachios also work, and those need to soak for only 4 to 6 hours.

NUT BUTTERS

Making your own nut butters is easy and gives you lots of flexibility to experiment with different combinations that you can't buy in the store, such as almond–cashew–Brazil nut butter. You can even add spices like ginger, cardamom, and cinnamon. Put any type of nut you like (roasted or unroasted) in a food processor. Depending on the quality of the food processor, you may need to add a tablespoon or two of nut oil to help them grind into a smooth puree. Refrigerate nut and seed butters in sealed containers for up to 2 months.

NUT OILS

There are two different categories of nut oils: toasted and untoasted. Toasted nut oils have a strong and robust nutty flavor, which we love in our salad dressings and sauces. However, they have a much shorter shelf life than untoasted nut oils and should be stored in the refrigerator after opening. Untoasted nut oils are a great option for cooking. Use almond oil for high heat (up to 495°F/257°C), walnut oil for medium-high heat (365 to 400°F/186 to 204°C), and peanut oil for medium heat (280 to 350°F/138 to 177°C).

Chapter 5

ENTREES

SEARED POLENTA *with* SPICY HEIRLOOM TOMATO SAUCE

This dish will warm your soul and win the hearts of your favorite omnivores. A plate of crispy pan-fried polenta cakes topped with heirloom tomato sauce is an entree to satisfy even the pickiest eater (and it's certified kid-friendly by my cousin, Nina Harmer). This dish is special to our whole family. We all adore the tomato sauce, a recipe my mom developed long before we decided to write this cookbook together, and we make it with tomatoes my dad grows in our garden. The polenta cooks quickly, but it needs an hour or two to cool in the fridge, so we recommend making it ahead of time or letting it cool while you cook the tomato sauce. Topped with toasted pine nuts and fresh parsley, my mom's sauce pairs perfectly with my seared polenta cakes—making this recipe an example of our creative mother-daughter collaboration.   —MAREA

Serves 4 as an entree or 8 as a side dish

POLENTA

2 cups/480 ml plain unsweetened soymilk

2 tbsp extra-virgin olive oil

1 tsp dried oregano

1 tsp salt

½ tsp freshly ground black pepper

½ tsp garlic powder

¼ tsp red pepper flakes

1 cup/175 g corn grits/polenta

¼ cup/35 g whole-wheat pastry flour or corn flour

Canola oil for frying

Spicy Heirloom Tomato Sauce (page 125) or good-quality jarred marinara sauce, heated

1 cup/30 g chopped fresh flat-leaf parsley

½ cup/60 g pine nuts, toasted (see page 117)

Grease a 9-by-9-in/23-by-23-cm baking pan with olive oil. Set aside.

To make the polenta: Combine the soymilk, olive oil, oregano, salt, pepper, garlic powder, red pepper flakes, and 2 cups/480 ml water in a medium saucepan, and bring them to a simmer over medium heat. At the same time, bring a second pot of water to a boil. Slowly whisk the polenta into the soymilk–olive oil mixture in the medium saucepan. Continue whisking until the mixture is smooth, reducing the heat to low to avoid spattering. Cook until the polenta grains are tender, about 15 minutes, whisking regularly (it should have the consistency of cream of wheat). If it gets very thick before the polenta is fully cooked, add additional boiling water, ¼ cup/60 ml at a time. Immediately pour the polenta into the prepared pan. Cool for about 20 minutes, then refrigerate until the polenta is cool, 1 to 2 hours.

Cut the cold polenta into eight equal triangles using a sharp knife. First cut a vertical line down the middle, followed by a horizontal line that divides the polenta into four equal squares. Then make two diagonal cuts from corner to corner to create eight triangles.

Sprinkle the flour on a flat plate and dredge each polenta triangle in flour. Ready a plate lined with several layers of paper towels.

continued

Place a large skillet (preferably cast iron) over medium-high heat and film it with a thin layer of canola oil. Sear the polenta triangles on each side until they are crispy and golden brown, about 5 minutes. Add more oil as needed between batches.

Transfer the seared polenta to the paper towel–lined plate to absorb excess oil.

To assemble the dish, place two polenta triangles on each plate. Top with hot tomato sauce. Sprinkle with the parsley and pine nuts, and serve immediately.

1 SERVING (2 POLENTA TRIANGLES PLUS ¼ OF THE SAUCE): CALORIES: 620 | FAT: 33G | CARBS: 73G | PROTEIN: 19G | SODIUM: 1120MG | DIETARY FIBER: 52% | POTASSIUM: 60% | VITAMIN A: 110% | VITAMIN C: 310% | VITAMIN E: 30% | THIAMIN: 30% | NIACIN: 30% | VITAMIN B$_6$: 35% | FOLATE: 35% | IRON: 50% | COPPER: 40% | PHOSPHORUS: 25% | MAGNESIUM: 30%

SPICY HEIRLOOM TOMATO SAUCE

Growing up in New York City, I had tomatoes that were hard, cold, tasteless wedges on iceberg lettuce salads. The first time I saw, smelled, and tasted a vine-ripened heirloom tomato, I was beside myself with joy. Miraculous! It took growing and having more heirloom tomatoes than we could possibly eat fresh to enable me to cook them into a sauce. Homemade heirloom tomato sauce turns the simplest pasta night into a gourmet dinner. I am so lucky because my husband, Drew, has become an avid tomato gardener, and he makes huge batches of sauce that we freeze in zip-top bags so we can enjoy the taste of peak summer all year long. This version is the Goodman classic sauce with a little extra kick from red pepper flakes to spice it up a bit. It's the perfect accompaniment to Marea's delectable seared polenta cakes. If you plan on doubling or tripling this recipe, you'll want to peel the tomatoes first (see Note). Otherwise, you can do what I usually do, and use tongs to pick the skins out of the sauce as it simmers. Marea doesn't mind the skins, and just leaves them in her sauce. The choice is yours.   —MYRA

Serves 4

3 tbsp olive oil, plus more for the baking dish

1 large yellow onion, coarsely chopped

2½ tbsp chopped garlic

¾ tsp red pepper flakes

6 lb/2.7 kg ripe heirloom tomatoes (quartered if you are not peeling them)

¼ cup plus 2 tbsp/90 ml tomato paste

Salt

Freshly ground black pepper

¾ cup/25 g packed chopped fresh basil

Heat the oil in a large, nonreactive pot over medium heat. Add the onion and cook, stirring frequently, until it softens but does not brown, 8 to 10 minutes. Add the garlic and red pepper flakes and cook, stirring frequently, another 2 minutes. Stir in the tomatoes, cover the pot, and cook, stirring frequently, until the tomatoes are soft, about 10 minutes. Using a potato masher, mash the tomatoes to break up the chunks. Add the tomato paste and ½ tsp salt and simmer, uncovered, stirring frequently, until the sauce thickens to the desired consistency, 30 to 45 minutes. Season with salt and pepper. Add the basil and simmer for 2 minutes more. Remove the pot from the heat. The sauce can be refrigerated, covered, for up to 1 week, and frozen for up to 1 year.

NOTE: PEELING TOMATOES

Cut a small X in the bottom of each tomato. Fill a large bowl with ice and water and set aside. Fill a large pot with water and bring it to a boil over high heat. Add four or five tomatoes to the pot and cook until the skins begin to wrinkle and split, 30 to 90 seconds. Using tongs or a slotted spoon, transfer the tomatoes to the bowl of ice water. Let the water in the pot return to a boil, and continue blanching the remaining tomatoes in small batches. If the water in the bowl gets warm, add more ice. When the tomatoes are cool enough to handle, pull off the skins with your fingers; they should come off easily.

1 SERVING: CALORIES: 250 | FAT: 12G | CARBS: 30G | PROTEIN: 9G | SODIUM: 530MG | DIETARY FIBER: 20% | POTASSIUM: 53% | VITAMIN A: 110% | VITAMIN C: 310% | VITAMIN E: 25% | THIAMIN: 20% | NIACIN: 25% | VITAMIN B$_6$: 35% | FOLATE: 30% | IRON: 35% | COPPER: 15% | PHOSPHORUS: 25% | MAGNESIUM: 20%

PASTA PUTTANESCA *with* GREEN *and* BLACK OLIVES

I love olives in my pasta sauce, so I've added two kinds to this puttanesca sauce, making it more original and flavorful. I've also added a splash of red wine, which isn't a traditional ingredient, but I think it should be. This is a wonderful dish any time of year, but during the summer, you can bring the fresh taste of the season to your table by substituting vine-ripe tomatoes for the whole canned ones, and adding a handful of chopped basil right before serving. My family's preferred pasta for this sauce is usually whole-wheat shells, but we also like rigatoni, penne, and linguine.   —MYRA

Serves 4

3 tbsp extra-virgin olive oil

1 large yellow onion, chopped

4 large garlic cloves, finely chopped

¼ tsp red pepper flakes

One 28-oz/800-g can whole, peeled Roma tomatoes, broken up into pieces, with juices

One 14.5-oz/415-g can crushed or diced tomatoes, with juices

2 tbsp red wine

¾ cup/105 g chopped kalamata olives

½ cup/70 g coarsely chopped green salad olives (without pimientos)

3 tbsp brined capers, drained

Salt

Freshly ground black pepper

½ cup/15 g packed chopped fresh flat-leaf parsley

1 lb/455 g dried pasta, such as whole-wheat shells, rigatoni, or linguine

Heat the oil in a large saucepan over medium heat. Add the onion and cook, stirring frequently, until it is soft, about 8 minutes. Add the garlic and red pepper flakes and cook, stirring constantly, for 2 minutes. Add the Roma tomatoes and the crushed tomatoes, with their juices. Reduce the heat to medium-low, stir in the wine, and simmer, covered, for 10 minutes.

Add the kalamata and green olives and continue to simmer the sauce, uncovered, for an additional 10 minutes. Add the capers and ½ tsp salt, and season with pepper. Cook for an additional 2 minutes, then stir in the parsley.

Meanwhile, bring a large pot of water to a boil over high heat. Add 1 tsp salt and the pasta. Cook according to package directions, until the pasta is al dente. Drain the pasta and transfer it to a large bowl. Add the sauce, tossing to coat. Alternatively, place the pasta on individual plates and top with the sauce. Serve hot.

1 SERVING: CALORIES: 560 | FAT: 18G | CARBS: 92G | PROTEIN: 18G | SODIUM: 910MG | DIETARY FIBER: 48% | POTASSIUM: 31% | VITAMIN A: 45% | VITAMIN C: 140% | VITAMIN E: 10% | THIAMIN: 40% | RIBOFLAVIN: 15% | NIACIN: 30% | VITAMIN B$_6$: 30% | FOLATE: 30% | CALCIUM: 15% | IRON: 40% | COPPER: 40% | PHOSPHORUS: 35% | MAGNESIUM: 40%

PASTA *with* CREAMY MUSHROOM SAUCE

Pasta with mushroom sauce is one of my husband's favorite dishes, so I was highly motivated to come up with a delicious version that is dairy-free. And voilà! Drew and I are thrilled with the result. This sauce goes well with either white or whole-wheat pasta, so typically we choose whole wheat for the added flavor, fiber, and vitamins. In fact, one serving of this recipe boasts 17 g protein, 52 percent of your daily fiber, and 30 percent of your iron. Fettuccine or penne are our preferred choices, but this works with virtually every type of pasta—and even polenta (see page 123). —MYRA

Serves 6

3 cups/720 ml Easy Vegetable Stock (page 76) or low-sodium vegetable or mushroom broth

1 oz/30 g dried porcini mushrooms

5½ tbsp/80 ml olive oil

1 large yellow onion, chopped

1 lb/455 g cremini or button mushrooms, bottoms trimmed and thinly sliced

2 large garlic cloves, coarsely chopped

½ tsp dried thyme

⅔ cup/165 ml dry white wine

Salt

Freshly ground black pepper

2½ tbsp unbleached, all-purpose flour

1¼ to 1½ cups/300 to 360 ml plain, unsweetened soymilk

½ cup/15 g packed chopped fresh flat-leaf parsley, plus more for garnishing (optional)

1 lb/455 g dried whole-wheat pasta

Bring the stock to a boil in a small saucepan. Remove it from the heat and stir in the porcini. Let them sit, covered, for 20 to 30 minutes, until the mushrooms are rehydrated. Strain the liquid through cheesecloth or a coffee filter to remove all the small particles. Keep the liquid warm and cut the porcini into bite-size pieces.

Place 3 tbsp of the oil in a large skillet over medium heat. Add the onion and cook, stirring frequently, until it begins to soften, about 5 minutes. Add the cremini and porcini mushrooms, cover the skillet, and cook for 10 minutes, stirring occasionally. Stir in the garlic and thyme and cook, uncovered, for 2 minutes. Add the wine and sauté, stirring occasionally, until the liquid evaporates. Season with ½ tsp salt and pepper.

In a small saucepan, heat the remaining 2½ tbsp oil over medium heat. Slowly whisk in the flour and cook, whisking constantly, until the flour just begins to darken slightly, about 3 minutes. Gradually add the warm porcini soaking liquid, whisking constantly until the sauce thickens and reaches the start of a simmer.

Add the sauce to the mushroom mixture and stir to blend. Heat the mixture over medium heat and slowly add 1¼ cups/300 ml of the soymilk. Cook until the sauce has thickened slightly and is hot, adding more soymilk if the sauce needs thinning. Stir in the parsley. Remove the skillet from the heat and season with salt and pepper.

Meanwhile, bring a large pot of water to a boil over high heat. Add 1 tsp salt and the pasta. Cook according to package directions, until the pasta is al dente. Drain the pasta and transfer it to a large bowl. Add the sauce, tossing to coat. Alternatively, place the pasta on individual plates and top with the sauce. Garnish with chopped parsley, if using. Serve immediately.

1 SERVING: CALORIES: 490 | FAT: 15G | CARBS: 73G | PROTEIN: 17G | SODIUM: 225MG | DIETARY FIBER: 52% | POTASSIUM: 19% | VITAMIN A: 15% | VITAMIN C: 20% | THIAMIN: 35% | RIBOFLAVIN: 30% | NIACIN: 35% | VITAMIN B$_6$: 15% | FOLATE: 20% | IRON: 30% | COPPER: 40% | PHOSPHORUS: 30% | MAGNESIUM: 30% | ZINC: 20%

SUMMER PESTO PIZZA

My husband is usually the pizza chef in our family, and he's very particular about what he likes, so I was a little nervous serving him this version without any cheese. Happily for us all, he absolutely loved it. Thin slices of zucchini stand in for mozzarella, while onions, kalamata olives, pine nuts, pesto, and fresh basil give it more than ample flavor and variety. One good-size zucchini yields the perfect amount of slices to cover the pizza, but if you have access to small yellow and green zucchini, little rounds of assorted colors would be lovely. Good-quality store-bought marinara sauce works just fine, but if you use our Spicy Heirloom Tomato Sauce, it makes this pizza extraordinary.

   My recipe for pesto makes 1 cup/240 ml, and you need only about half of it for the pizza, but I believe if you are going to dirty the food processor, you should make enough pesto for a pasta dinner later in the week. While fresh pizza dough from the market works great, I've included a recipe for 100% Whole-Wheat Pizza Dough, which is fun to make from scratch if you have the time. It's hard to find all-whole-wheat pizza dough at the market, and fresh dough is especially fun to make if you are cooking with kids.   —MYRA

Serves 3 to 4; makes one 14-in/35.5-cm pizza

Whole-wheat pastry flour for rolling out the dough

One ball 100% Whole-Wheat Pizza Dough (page 131) or 1 lb/455 g store-bought dough

Cornmeal for dusting

2 tbsp extra-virgin olive oil

¾ cup/180 ml good-quality marinara sauce or Spicy Heirloom Tomato Sauce (page 125)

1 large zucchini, thinly sliced

1 medium yellow onion, cut in half lengthwise, then cut crosswise into eight slices

½ cup/70 g pitted kalamata olives, coarsely chopped

Position a rack on the bottom of the oven and if using a pizza stone, place it on the rack. Preheat the oven to 500°F/260°C/gas 10 for at least 30 minutes so that the stone is hot.

Lightly flour a work surface and a rolling pin. Shape the dough by patting it into a flat, round disk. Then roll it out on the work surface to form a 14-in/40.5-cm round, ⅛ to ¼ in/3 to 6 mm thick. If your pizza stone is smaller than this, adjust accordingly.

If using a pizza peel or pizza pan, generously dust it with cornmeal (alternatively, use a large baking sheet and dust it with cornmeal).

Transfer the dough to the prepared pizza peel, pan, or baking sheet. Brush the dough lightly with about 1 tbsp of the oil, leaving a ¾-in/ 2-cm border unoiled.

Cover the dough with a thin layer of tomato sauce. Arrange the zucchini slices in concentric circles on the dough, leaving the ¾-in/2-cm border bare. Arrange the onion atop the zucchini, and then scatter the olives over the dough.

Slide the pizza off the peel and onto the preheated stone, using a jerking motion to release it. (Alternatively, place the pizza pan or baking sheet in the oven.) Bake for 8 minutes.

Check to see that the pizza is cooking evenly, rotating it if necessary. Continue cooking until the crust is golden brown and the toppings are sizzling hot, 3 to 5 minutes more.

continued

PESTO

4 cups/120 g packed fresh basil

½ cup/120 ml extra-virgin olive oil

¼ cup/30 g pine nuts, toasted (see page 117)

1 tbsp coarsely chopped fresh garlic

¼ tsp salt

TOPPINGS

2 tbsp pine nuts, toasted (see page 117)

¼ cup/10 g packed thinly sliced fresh basil

Garlic powder (optional)

Red pepper flakes (optional)

Meanwhile, make the pesto: Put the basil, oil, pine nuts, garlic, and salt in a food processor and pulse until coarsely chopped, then puree until the mixture is smooth, stopping to scrape the sides of the bowl with a rubber spatula as needed. If not using immediately, cover and store for up to 2 weeks in the refrigerator. Return the pesto to room temperature before using.

Remove the pizza from the oven by sliding the peel under it, or use tongs to slide the pizza off the stone onto a cutting board. (If using a pizza pan or baking sheet, remove the entire pan from the oven and transfer the pizza onta a cutting board.) Using half the pesto, immediately drop teaspoons of pesto all over the top. Spread it over the topping with the back of a spoon or with a cake spatula. Sprinkle with the pine nuts and basil.

Using a sharp knife or a pizza cutter, cut the pizza into eight slices, and serve them hot with garlic powder and red pepper flakes, if using.

2 SLICES: CALORIES: 470 | FAT: 29G | CARBS: 48G | PROTEIN: 8G | SODIUM: 900MG | DIETARY FIBER: 36% | VITAMIN A: 45% | VITAMIN C: 25% | VITAMIN E: 10% | THIAMIN: 15% | RIBOFLAVIN: 10% | NIACIN: 20% | VITAMIN B$_6$: 20% | FOLATE: 20% | CALCIUM: 15% | IRON: 25% | COPPER: 25% | PHOSPHORUS: 15% | MAGNESIUM: 20% | ZINC: 10%

Variation: FALAFEL PIZZA

Make the falafel, salad, and sauce from our Baked Falafel Pitas with Chopped Greek Salad and Roasted Cashew Sauce (page 146). Brush rolled-out pizza dough with 1 tbsp olive oil mixed with 1 large pressed garlic clove. Bake the dough in a preheated 500°F/260°C/gas 10 oven for about 10 minutes, until the crust just begins to turn golden. Remove the crust and top with bite-size pieces of falafel, and return to the oven for another 2 minutes or so, until the falafel is warmed through and the crust is golden brown and crispy. Generously drizzle the pizza with the cashew sauce, and then top with the Greek Salad. Serve immediately.

100% WHOLE-WHEAT PIZZA DOUGH

When I have the time, I always enjoy making homemade pizza dough. I love kneading the dough, watching it rise, punching it down, and rolling it out. One hundred percent whole-grain pizza dough is hard to find, and this one is delicious and plenty light. I particularly like the chewy flecks of bulgur in this version, which makes it even more tasty and unique. This dough freezes well, so making a batch is a great investment for future meals.   —MYRA

Makes three 14-in/35.5-cm pizzas

¼ cup/40 g bulgur

1 cup/240 ml boiling water

1 tbsp plus 1 tsp active dry yeast

1 tbsp sugar

¼ cup/60 ml extra-virgin olive oil

2 tsp salt

1¾ cups/230 g whole-wheat flour

1¾ cups/245 g whole-wheat pastry flour

Combine the bulgur with the boiling water in a small bowl and cover with a plate to keep warm. Let sit for 10 minutes to soften.

Meanwhile, in a large bowl, combine 1½ cups/360 ml warm water (105 to 115°F/40 to 45°C) with the yeast and sugar. Whisk to combine and let the mixture rest until it is foamy, about 5 minutes.

Drain the bulgur in a fine-mesh sieve, discarding the water. Add the bulgur to the yeast mixture along with the oil and salt. Stir in 1 cup/120 g of the whole-wheat flour and 1 cup/120 g of the whole-wheat pastry flour. Whisk vigorously for 2 to 3 minutes.

Stir in the remaining ¾ cup/90 g of both flours. Lightly flour a work surface with whole-wheat pastry flour. Transfer the dough to the prepared work surface and knead it until smooth and elastic, about 5 minutes.

Oil a large bowl. Place the dough in the bowl and turn it so that it is lightly coated with the oil. Cover the bowl with a towel, and let the dough rise in a warm, draft-free place until it doubles in size, about 1 hour.

Gently punch down the dough to deflate it, cover the bowl, and let it rise again until doubled in size, 30 to 45 minutes. Divide the dough into three balls and you're ready to make pizza. If you are making only one pizza, you can wrap two balls in plastic wrap and freeze them for up to 2 months. The balls defrost in the fridge overnight or on the kitchen counter in about 2 hours. Bring the dough to room temperature before using.

1 SERVING (⅛ OF ONE PIZZA DOUGH): CALORIES: 170 | FAT: 5G | CARBS: 28G | PROTEIN: 5G | SODIUM: 390MG | DIETARY FIBER: 20%

TERIYAKI TOFU BROCCOLETTE *on* WILD RICE

With homemade teriyaki sauce, pan-fried tofu, sautéed red bell pepper, broccolette, and hearty wild rice, this stir-fry has it all. This recipe makes extra teriyaki sauce, because I love to have this sauce in my fridge to serve over veggies or rice. Broccolette is a delicious, hearty vegetable that is packed with vitamins and minerals. A cross between broccoli and Chinese kale, it's subtly sweet and tastes almost like asparagus. It's also known as broccolini and baby broccoli. If you've never tried it before, this is a perfect introduction to the magic of broccolette. —MAREA

Serves 4

WILD RICE

1 cup/190 g wild rice, rinsed

1½ tsp extra virgin olive oil

¼ tsp salt

¼ tsp ground cumin

TERIYAKI SAUCE

¾ cup/180 ml low-sodium soy sauce

¼ cup plus 2 tbsp/75 g packed brown sugar

2 tbsp unseasoned rice vinegar

1 tbsp plus 1 tsp finely minced, peeled fresh ginger

1 tbsp plus 1 tsp finely minced garlic

⅛ tsp red pepper flakes

STIR-FRY

14 oz/400 g firm tofu, medium dice

4 tbsp/60 ml high-heat oil, such as safflower

1 small yellow onion, small dice

1 medium red bell pepper, small dice

5 cups/350 g medium-dice broccolette

Sesame seeds for garnishing

To make the rice: Combine the rice, oil, salt, and cumin with 2 cups/ 480 ml of water in a medium saucepan. Place the pan over high heat and bring to a boil. Reduce the heat to maintain a simmer and cook, covered, until the rice is tender and there is no water left in the pot, about 1 hour. If the rice is cooked and there is still liquid left in the pan, drain the rice.

Meanwhile, make the teriyaki sauce: Combine the soy sauce, sugar, vinegar, ginger, garlic, red pepper flakes, and ½ cup/120 ml water in a small, heavy-bottomed saucepan over medium-high heat. Bring to the start of a boil, and then reduce the heat to low and simmer, uncovered, until the sauce thickens slightly, about 10 minutes. Remove the pan from the heat and let the sauce sit at room temperature while you prepare the remaining ingredients.

To make the stir-fry: Place the tofu cubes on a clean kitchen towel and let them drain, about 5 minutes. Transfer the tofu to a medium mixing bowl and add ½ cup/120 ml of the teriyaki sauce, stirring to thoroughly coat all surfaces. Marinate the tofu at room temperature for at least 15 minutes. Transfer it to a sieve set over a bowl and drain; reserve the marinade.

Add 2 tbsp of the high-heat oil to a large skillet over medium-high heat. Arrange the tofu in a single layer and cook, flipping it gently, until all sides are crispy and brown, about 5 minutes. Transfer the tofu to the bowl with the reserved marinade. Cover with a plate and set aside at room temperature.

continued

Return the skillet to the stove over medium-high heat. Add the remaining 2 tbsp of the oil and cook the onion, stirring frequently, until it lightly browns, about 3 minutes. Add the bell pepper and cook until it softens slightly, 3 to 5 minutes. Stir in the broccolette and cook, stirring frequently, until the stems are crisp-tender, about 5 minutes. Add the reserved tofu and its marinade to the skillet and stir to combine. Cook until the mixture is hot, 1 to 2 minutes, adding additional teriyaki sauce to taste.

Place about ¾ cup/130 g of wild rice on each plate. Top with 1½ cups/255 g of the vegetable mixture. Sprinkle with sesame seeds and serve immediately.

1 SERVING (USING ⅔ OF THE TERIYAKI SAUCE): CALORIES: 400 | FAT: 21G | CARBS: 39G | PROTEIN: 18G | SODIUM: 1,350MG | DIETARY FIBER: 16% | VITAMIN A: 60% | VITAMIN C: 260% | VITAMIN E: 15% | NIACIN: 10% | VITAMIN B$_6$: 20% | FOLATE: 10% | CALCIUM: 30% | IRON: 25% | COPPER: 20% | ZINC: 15%

LENTIL *and* POTATO CURRY

For most Americans, the bold taste of curry powder represents the distinctive flavor of Indian cuisine. So you might be surprised to learn that the commercial blends we buy in the supermarket are virtually unknown in India. Instead of packaged spice blends, many households develop their own signature curries from a wide array of seeds and powders. I used commercial curry powder in my early version of this recipe, until I was encouraged by Marabeth Karmally, who makes magical Indian food, to try creating a spice mix from scratch. Who knew it would be so easy and would make this dish extra delicious? Small amounts of seeds and aromatics are slowly sautéed, a technique that coaxes a nuanced complexity of aromas and flavors from the ingredients. The subtle interplay of spices enhances (rather than overwhelms) the vegetables. We included carrots and peas, which is not traditional, because we like adding their slight sweetness and bright color. —MYRA

Serves 4

2 tbsp extra-virgin olive oil

1 large yellow onion, medium dice

4 dried red chile peppers, about 2 in/5 cm long

¼ tsp black mustard seeds

¼ tsp cumin seeds

2 large tomatoes, chopped (peeling optional; see page 125)

½ cup/90 g split red lentils, rinsed

½ cup/100 g French green lentils, rinsed

4 cups/960 ml very hot water (about 180°F/82°C)

2 jalapeño peppers, finely chopped, seeds and ribs optional

3 large garlic cloves, chopped

1 tbsp finely minced, peeled fresh ginger

1½ tsp salt

¼ tsp ground turmeric

1 lb/455 g Yukon Gold or Yellow Finn potatoes, medium dice

1 large carrot, thinly sliced

1 cup/130 g fresh or frozen peas

Cooked brown basmati rice

Heat the oil in a large skillet over medium heat. Add the onion, red chiles, mustard seeds, and cumin seeds and cook, stirring frequently, until the onion is soft and has begun to turn golden brown, about 15 minutes. Add the tomatoes and cook, stirring frequently, until they soften and break down, 3 to 5 minutes. Set aside.

Put the red and green lentils and hot water in a large saucepan over high heat. Bring to the start of a simmer, and reduce the heat to medium-low. Add the onion-spice mixture, the jalapeños, garlic, ginger, salt, and turmeric. Cover the pan and simmer for 5 minutes. Add the potatoes and simmer, covered, for 9 minutes. Stir in the carrot, cover the pan, and continue cooking until the vegetables are crisptender, about 8 minutes more.

Remove the cover and stir in the peas. Cook until the peas are hot, the lentils are just tender, and most of the liquid has been absorbed, about 5 minutes. If the liquid has evaporated, add ½ cup/120 ml of hot water.

Serve hot over brown basmati rice.

1 SERVING (CURRY ONLY): CALORIES: 490 | FAT: 10G | CARBS: 80G | PROTEIN: 20G | SODIUM: 1,560MG | DIETARY FIBER: 52% | POTASSIUM: 24% | VITAMIN A: 170% | VITAMIN C: 140% | THIAMIN: 20% | VITAMIN B$_6$: 20% | FOLATE: 15% | IRON: 30% | COPPER: 15% | PHOSPHORUS: 15% | MAGNESIUM: 15%

GRILLED SUMMER VEGETABLES *and* TOFU *on* SWEET CORN *and* FARRO

When summer days are long and warm, grilling outside often feels like the right thing to do. I love this dish, created in collaboration with Earthbound Farm's chef Sarah LaCasse, because it features many of my favorite ingredients: chewy whole grains of farro, sweet corn, and sweet-tart grilled cherry tomatoes. —MYRA

Serves 4

FARRO

1 cup/180 g farro (see page 186)

½ tsp salt

TOFU

1¼ tsp salt

1 tsp pure ground chipotle chile

1 tsp ground cumin

½ tsp sweet paprika

½ tsp freshly ground black pepper

¼ tsp dried thyme

¼ tsp dried oregano

¼ tsp garlic powder

1 lb/455 g extra-firm tofu

Cooking spray or canola oil

5 tbsp olive oil

1 tbsp fresh lemon juice

2 tsp red wine vinegar

½ tsp dried oregano

Salt

Freshly ground black pepper

4 small zucchini, cut into thirds lengthwise

16 cherry tomatoes

2 large ears corn, shucked

1 tsp chopped garlic

Pinch of dried oregano

Preheat a grill to cook directly on medium-high. Soak four 6-in/15-cm wooden skewers for 10 minutes in cold water.

To make the farro: Combine 2 cups/480 ml water, the farro, and salt in a small saucepan. Cover and bring to a boil over high heat. Reduce the heat to maintain a simmer and cook, covered, for 20 minutes. Remove from the heat and set aside (covered) until the water is fully absorbed, 5 to 10 minutes.

To make the tofu: In a small bowl, stir together the salt, chipotle chile, cumin, paprika, pepper, thyme, oregano, and garlic powder. Cut the tofu into rectangles that are about ½ in/12 mm thick. Depending on the shape of your tofu, cut either eight or twelve rectangles. Place the tofu on a plate and spray or brush both sides with oil. Sprinkle both sides as evenly as possible with the spice rub, pat it on to help it stick, and let sit for at least 10 minutes.

In a small bowl, combine 3 tbsp of the oil, the lemon juice, vinegar, oregano, ½ tsp salt, and ¼ tsp pepper. Brush the marinade over the zucchini pieces, cherry tomatoes, and corn.

Place the zucchini and corn directly on the grill, turning to cook all sides, until marked and the zucchini is tender when pierced with a fork, 4 to 5 minutes. Grill the tofu, turning once, until marked and warmed all the way through, 5 to 6 minutes. Thread 4 tomatoes on each skewer and grill, turning twice, until warm and the skins begin to burst, 2 to 3 minutes.

When the corn is cool enough to handle, cut the kernels off the cobs and add them to the farro. Add the garlic, remaining 2 tbsp oil, and a pinch each of salt, pepper, and oregano; toss to combine. Cut the zucchini in half crosswise. Place the farro-corn mixture on a serving platter or on individual plates. Place the zucchini and tofu slices on the farro, and top off with the skewered cherry tomatoes to serve.

1 SERVING: CALORIES: 540 | FAT: 28G | CARBS: 61G | PROTEIN: 22G | SODIUM: 760MG | DIETARY FIBER: 52% | POTASSIUM: 27% | VITAMIN A: 80% | VITAMIN C: 40% | VITAMIN E: 10% | THIAMIN: 20% | RIBOFLAVIN: 15% | NIACIN: 15% | VITAMIN B₆: 25% | FOLATE: 20% | CALCIUM: 30% | IRON: 50% | COPPER: 25% | PHOSPHORUS: 30% | MAGNESIUM: 35% | ZINC: 15%

MIDSUMMER RATATOUILLE *on* QUINOA

This simple dish is bursting with flavor and freshness and is such a satisfying meal. A traditional French vegetable stew, ratatouille is a medley of seasonal summer vegetables and herbs. It is best to make this recipe during the summer, when these vegetables are at their peak. If you're craving it in the winter, you can substitute canned tomatoes for fresh, since they are more flavorful when tomatoes are out of season. Served over quinoa, this ratatouille is one of my favorite summer dishes. —MAREA

Serves 4

QUINOA

2 cups/480 ml Easy Vegetable Stock (page 76), low-sodium vegetable broth, or water

1 cup/170 g quinoa

1 tsp dried oregano

½ tsp salt

RATATOUILLE

1 small eggplant, small dice

Salt

3 tbsp extra-virgin olive oil

1 large yellow onion, small dice

4 large garlic cloves, slivered

2 medium red bell peppers, small dice

1 tsp dried thyme

1 tsp dried oregano

Big pinch of red pepper flakes

2½ cups/150 g small-dice cremini mushrooms

2 medium zucchini, small dice

2 large tomatoes, small dice

½ cup/15 g minced fresh basil

3 tbsp minced fresh flat-leaf parsley

Freshly ground black pepper

To make the quinoa: Rinse the quinoa thoroughly in cold water. Combine the stock, quinoa, oregano, and salt in a medium pot over high heat. Cover the pot and bring to a boil, then reduce the heat to a simmer and cook, covered, stirring occasionally, until the quinoa is tender and all the water has evaporated, about 20 minutes.

To make the ratatouille: Toss the eggplant in a large mixing bowl with ¾ tsp salt. Set aside while you prepare the other ingredients.

Warm the oil in a large saucepan with a tight-fitting lid over medium heat. Add the onion and garlic and sauté until translucent and fragrant, about 5 minutes. Add the bell pepper, thyme, oregano, and red pepper flakes. Sauté for about 5 minutes, until the bell pepper is soft. Add the mushrooms. Cover and cook, stirring frequently, for 3 minutes. Add the eggplant and cook, covered, stirring frequently, for 3 minutes. Remove the lid and cook uncovered for another 3 minutes. Add the zucchini and sauté for about 5 minutes, until the zucchini is fully cooked. Add the tomatoes and cook uncovered for another 3 minutes, until all the flavors have melded together. Turn off the heat. Add the basil and parsley, and season with salt and pepper.

Divide the quinoa among four serving bowls, followed by a few scoops of ratatouille. Serve immediately.

1 SERVING: CALORIES: 260 | FAT: 12G | CARBS: 36G | PROTEIN: 7G | SODIUM: 750MG | DIETARY FIBER: 32% | POTASSIUM: 29% | VITAMIN A: 80% | VITAMIN C: 260% | VITAMIN E: 15% | THIAMIN: 20% | RIBOFLAVIN: 15% | NIACIN: 20% | VITAMIN B_6: 30% | FOLATE: 25% | IRON: 20% | COPPER: 30% | PHOSPHORUS: 20% | MAGNESIUM: 25% | ZINC: 10%

SLOW-SIMMERED BEANS *with* TUSCAN KALE *on* BULGUR

This recipe is one of my favorites. I often make a pot of slow-simmered beans to have waiting in the fridge as a snack or side dish. However, if I want to turn them into an official meal, I add sautéed kale and serve them over bulgur. Lima beans, great Northern beans, and cannellini also work well in this recipe, but try corona beans, if you can find them—they are extra large, buttery, and satisfying. Corona beans will need to soak longer, 12 to 24 hours, and they will also take about an hour longer to cook. If you prepare the beans a day or two ahead of time, this dish comes together quickly. Serve with a big salad, and this is a great meal. —MYRA

Serves 4

BEANS

2 cups/450 g dried beans, such as lima, great Northern, corona, or cannellini

6 cups/1.4 L Easy Vegetable Stock (page 76) or low-sodium vegetable broth

4 large garlic cloves, quartered

2 tbsp olive oil

1 tsp dried oregano

½ tsp dried thyme or 1½ tsp fresh thyme

1 bay leaf

Freshly ground black pepper

1 tsp salt

BULGUR

¾ tsp salt

1½ cups/255 g bulgur

1 tbsp olive oil

KALE

2 tbsp olive oil

3 large garlic cloves, slivered

3 cups/90 g destemmed and sliced dino (Tuscan) kale

Freshly ground black pepper

Salt

To make the beans: Rinse the beans and place them in a large bowl Cover with 6 to 8 cups/1.4 to 2 L water, and soak them for 8 hours (or at least 12 if using corona beans) or overnight.

Drain the beans and place them in a medium saucepan. Add the stock and bring it to the start of a boil over high heat. Add the garlic, oil, oregano, thyme, and bay leaf, season with pepper, and reduce the heat to low to maintain a slow simmer. Cook, covered, until the beans are very tender, about 2 hours. Be sure to keep the beans submerged in liquid while they cook, adding boiling water as necessary. When they are done, a modest amount of flavorful stock will have formed. Remove from heat, add the salt, and discard the bay leaf.

To make the bulgur: Bring 3 cups/720 ml water and the salt to a boil in a medium saucepan over high heat. Add the bulgur, return the mixture to a boil, and then reduce the heat to maintain a slow simmer. Simmer, covered, for 20 minutes, until the bulgur is tender and the water is absorbed. Remove from the heat and fluff the bulgur with a fork. Drizzle the oil over the bulgur and blend with a fork.

While the bulgur is cooking, prepare the kale: Warm the oil in a large skillet over medium heat. Stir in the garlic and kale. Cook, covered, stirring frequently, until the kale is tender, about 10 minutes. Season with pepper.

Add the kale to the saucepan with the beans and simmer for 3 minutes, or until the beans are warmed through. Season with salt and pepper, as needed. Serve over the hot bulgur.

1 SERVING: CALORIES: 370 | FAT: 19G | CARBS: 42G | PROTEIN: 10G | SODIUM: 1,660MG | DIETARY FIBER: 44% | VITAMIN A: 70% | FOLATE: 30% | CALCIUM: 20% | IRON: 25%

WHITE BEAN, BUTTERNUT SQUASH, *and*
BARLEY STEW *with* WHOLE-WHEAT BISCUITS

Have you ever noticed that a great meal somehow tastes even more delicious when you know it's especially healthy? That's a bonus for this hearty stew, where chewy barley, earthy chard, sweet parsnips, creamy butternut squash, and delicious white beans blend into a combination that is dense in flavor and in health benefits. I use hulled barley because it is the least processed and has the best nutrition, but pearled barley will work just fine. This stew feels like a decadent treat when served with flaky Whole-Wheat Biscuits (facing page). They are easy to make, but warm, toasted, crusty whole-wheat bread makes a good stand-in served with a bowl of good-quality olive oil sprinkled with a little sea salt for dipping. —MYRA

Serves 6

1 cup/200 g hulled barley, rinsed

6 cups/1.4 L Easy Vegetable Stock (page 76) or low-sodium vegetable stock

3 tbsp olive oil

2 medium yellow onions, medium dice

2 medium parsnips, medium dice

3 cups/420 g peeled medium-dice butternut squash

2 large garlic cloves, coarsely chopped

1 tsp dried thyme

1 tsp dried oregano

Freshly ground black pepper

1½ cups/255 g cooked cannellini beans (rinsed and drained if canned)

Salt

6 cups/180 g sliced rainbow or Swiss chard, stems thinly sliced, leaves medium sliced

2 tbsp fresh lemon juice

Whole-Wheat Biscuits (facing page)

Put the barley in a medium saucepan and add 3 cups/720 ml of the stock. Bring to a boil over high heat, then reduce the heat to maintain a simmer and cook, covered, for 40 minutes.

While the barley cooks, put the oil in a 6-qt/5.7-L pot over medium heat. Add the onions and cook, stirring occasionally, until they are translucent, about 5 minutes. Add the parsnips and squash and cook, stirring frequently, for 5 minutes. Add the garlic, thyme, and oregano, and season with pepper, then cook, stirring frequently, for 2 minutes. Stir in the remaining 3 cups/720 ml of the stock, the cooked barley, beans, and 1 tsp salt. Bring the mixture to a simmer and cook, covered, for 5 minutes, stirring regularly. Add the chard, cover, and cook for another 10 minutes. You can add up to 1 cup/240 ml hot water in ¼-cup/60-ml increments if there isn't enough liquid to keep the stew simmering.

Remove from the heat. Stir in the lemon juice and season with salt and pepper. Serve hot with biscuits.

1 SERVING (STEW ONLY): CALORIES: 340 | FAT: 8G | CARBS: 61G | PROTEIN: 10G | SODIUM: 500MG | DIETARY FIBER: 56% | POTASSIUM: 28% | VITAMIN A: 230% | VITAMIN C: 60% | VITAMIN E: 15% | THIAMIN: 45% | RIBOFLAVIN: 15% | NIACIN: 15% | VITAMIN B₆: 20% | FOLATE: 15% | CALCIUM: 15% | IRON: 20% | COPPER: 20% | PHOSPHORUS: 20% | MAGNESIUM: 35% | ZINC: 15%

WHOLE-WHEAT BISCUITS

It's hard to resist warm biscuits straight from the oven. We think they make a perfect complement to our stew or to Country Mashed Potatoes with Mushroom Gravy (page 169). While biscuits should be eaten fresh from the oven, our family gobbles up any leftover biscuits the next morning, served toasted with vegan "buttery" spread and raspberry jam.

Makes 16

1 cup/240 ml plain, unsweetened soymilk

1 tbsp white vinegar

2¼ cups/315 g whole-wheat pastry flour, plus more for dusting

2½ tsp baking powder

¾ tsp salt

½ tsp baking soda

½ cup/120 ml Earth Balance Buttery Spread or a similar product

Place a rack in the middle of the oven and preheat it to 450°F/230°C/gas 8. Lightly grease a baking sheet and set aside.

In a small bowl, whisk together the soymilk and vinegar. Let sit for 10 minutes to thicken into "buttermilk."

In a medium bowl, whisk together the flour, baking powder, salt, and baking soda. Add the Earth Balance to the flour mixture, using your fingers to mix it with the flour until well combined and crumbly.

Whisk the "buttermilk" and add it to the flour mixture. Stir until just combined.

Turn out the dough onto a floured surface and knead for only 20 seconds. This is a wet dough, so use enough flour to keep it from sticking. Flatten the dough into a round that is ¾ in/2 cm thick. Cut out circles with a 2¼- to 2½-in/5.5- to 6-cm cookie cutter or jar. Transfer the biscuits to the prepared pan and arrange them 1 in/2.5 cm apart. Combine the scraps of leftover dough and reflatten them, continuing to cut biscuits until all the dough is used.

Bake until the biscuits are golden brown and fragrant, 12 to 16 minutes. Serve warm.

1 BISCUIT: CALORIES: 120 | FAT: 6G | CARBS: 13G | PROTEIN: 2G | SODIUM: 290MG | DIETARY FIBER: 12%

FOUR BEAN *and* SWEET POTATO CHILI *with* SKILLET CORN BREAD

When I make pots of chili, I always think: The bigger, the better. And this recipe is both. It's Big—enough to feed your whole family, a group of friends, or to save for leftovers. And it's Better—bursting with hearty ingredients, including four different kinds of beans, sweet potato, corn, and plenty of other veggies and spices. The best way to serve this chili is with my mom's Skillet Corn Bread. It truly deserves a big yum.   —MAREA

Serves 8

¼ cup/60 ml ~~olive oil~~ *veg broth*

2 medium yellow onions, medium dice

2 large carrots, medium dice

2 medium red bell peppers, medium dice

1 jalapeño pepper, seeds and ribs discarded, finely chopped

4 large garlic cloves, finely chopped

1 tbsp plus 1 tsp ground cumin

1 tbsp plus 1 tsp dried oregano

2 tsp chili powder

1½ tsp sweet paprika

1½ tsp ground coriander

1½ tsp dried thyme

¼ tsp cayenne pepper

¼ tsp red pepper flakes

2 bay leaves

can combine

3 cups/720 ml Easy Vegetable *divided* Stock (page 76) or low-sodium vegetable stock

1 large sweet potato, peeling optional, medium dice

One 28-oz/800-g can diced tomatoes, or 3 large fresh tomatoes, diced, with juices

3 tbsp tomato paste

Heat the oil in a large stockpot over medium heat. Add the onions, carrots, bell peppers, jalapeño, and garlic. Cook, stirring frequently, until the vegetables are soft and fragrant, about 8 minutes. Stir in the cumin, oregano, chili powder, paprika, coriander, thyme, cayenne, red pepper flakes, and bay leaves. Cook, stirring constantly, for 1 to 2 minutes. Add the stock, sweet potato, tomatoes, and tomato paste. Cook, covered, over medium-low heat, stirring frequently, for 15 minutes. Remove the bay leaves before serving.

1½ cups/255 g cooked black beans (rinsed and drained if canned)

1½ cups/255 g cooked kidney beans (rinsed and drained if canned)

1½ cups/255 g cooked black-eyed peas (rinsed and drained if canned)

1½ cups/255 g cooked pinto beans (rinsed and drained if canned)

3 cups/420 g fresh or frozen (thawed) corn

⅓ cup/15 g minced fresh flat-leaf parsley

1 tbsp red wine vinegar

Salt

Freshly ground black pepper

1 cup/90 g thinly sliced green onions, green and white parts, for garnishing

Skillet Corn Bread (page 144)

Add the black beans, kidney beans, black-eyed peas, and pinto beans and continue cooking, covered, until the chili thickens and the sweet potato is tender. Add the corn and cook, uncovered, for 5 minutes. Stir in the parsley and vinegar and remove the pan from the heat.

Season the chili with salt and pepper and serve immediately, garnished with the green onions, and a wedge of corn bread on the side.

1 SERVING (CHILI ONLY): CALORIES: 360 | FAT: 9G | CARBS: 62G | PROTEIN: 13G | SODIUM: 690MG | DIETARY FIBER: 80% | POTASSIUM: 32% | VITAMIN A: 370% | VITAMIN C: 150% | VITAMIN E: 15% | THIAMIN: 25% | RIBOFLAVIN: 15% | NIACIN: 15% | VITAMIN B$_6$: 30% | FOLATE: 40% | CALCIUM: 15% | IRON: 30% | COPPER: 25% | PHOSPHORUS: 25% | MAGNESIUM: 30% | ZINC: 15%

SKILLET CORN BREAD

Clearly, corn bread is the perfect complement for chili—but why limit its appeal? I love corn bread with salads, for breakfast with almond butter, or just as a snack anytime. This quick and easy recipe features all whole grains and is just a little bit sweet. Baking in a skillet creates a wonderfully crispy crust and also provides a rustic serving dish that keeps the corn bread warm through the meal. If you don't own a cast-iron skillet, you can use a baking pan and it will still taste great. —MYRA

Serves ~~12~~ 8

pie
use stone

1½ cups/360 ml plain, unsweetened soymilk

1½ tbsp fresh lemon juice

2 tbsp ground flaxseed

¼ cup very hot water (about 180°F/82°C)

⅓ cup/75 ml canola oil

¼ cup/60 ml pure maple syrup

1 tbsp sugar

1¾ cups/265 g yellow cornmeal, medium grind

1¼ cups/175 g whole-wheat pastry flour

1½ tsp baking powder

½ tsp baking soda

½ tsp salt

1 tbsp high-heat oil, such as safflower

Position a rack in the middle of the oven and preheat it to 450°F/230°C/gas 8. Place a 10-in/25-cm cast-iron skillet in the oven as it preheats. (If you are making the corn bread in a baking pan, preheat the oven to 400°F/200°C/gas 6. Grease the bottom and sides of a 9-by-9-in/23-by-23-cm baking pan and set aside.)

In a large mixing bowl, whisk together the soymilk and lemon juice. Let the mixture sit for 5 to 10 minutes to thicken into "buttermilk."

In a small bowl, combine the flaxseed with the hot water. Allow to sit for 5 to 10 minutes until it thickens (this is our egg substitute). Whisk the flaxseed mixture and add it to the "buttermilk" along with the canola oil, syrup, and sugar.

In a medium mixing bowl, whisk together the cornmeal, flour, baking powder, baking soda, and salt. Add the dry mixture to the wet mixture, stirring until just combined. Do not overmix.

Remove the hot skillet and add the high-heat oil. Swirl the pan so that the oil coats all surfaces, making sure it goes at least 1½ in/4 cm up the sides. Pour in the batter. It will sizzle. (If you are making the corn bread in a baking pan, transfer the batter to the prepared pan.)

Bake for 10 minutes, and then lower the oven temperature to 350°F/180°C/gas 4, and continue to bake for 10 to 15 minutes, or until the corn bread is golden brown, firm to the touch, and a toothpick inserted in the middle comes out clean. (If using a baking pan, continue to bake for 20 minutes, or until the bread has pulled away from the sides of the pan and a toothpick inserted in the middle comes out clean.)

Serve the corn bread right in the cast-iron pan to keep it warm, but warn everyone that the pan is hot! (If you've made the corn bread in a baking pan, let the pan cool on a wire rack for 10 minutes, then cut the bread into twelve rectangles and serve warm.)

1 SLICE: CALORIES: 220 | FAT: 9G | CARBS: 30G | PROTEIN: 4G | SODIUM: 160MG | DIETARY FIBER: 16% | IRON: 10% | PHOSPHORUS: 10%

BAKED FALAFEL PITAS *with* CHOPPED GREEK SALAD *and* ROASTED CASHEW SAUCE

I consider this more than a recipe, even more than a meal; it's an explosion of unique flavors that truly do enhance each other. The combination of savory baked falafels, Greek salad, and exquisite roasted cashew sauce makes a falafel pita that's hard to beat—and harder to resist. I recommend preparing the salad and sauce first, so the falafels are ready to serve as soon as they come out of the oven. Served with Quinoa Tabbouleh (page 68), this dish will feed eight people. For a change from traditional falafel pitas, this recipe transforms into an amazing falafel pizza (see page 131). —MAREA

Serves 4 to 8

CHOPPED GREEK SALAD

2 medium cucumbers, seeding and peeling optional, small dice

2 cups/300 g tomatoes (vine-ripened, heirloom, or cherry or pear tomatoes), small dice

⅓ cup/15 g packed finely chopped fresh flat-leaf parsley

⅓ cup/15 g packed finely chopped fresh cilantro

¼ cup/25 g finely diced red onion

2 tbsp fresh lemon juice

1 tbsp extra-virgin olive oil

Salt

Freshly ground black pepper

ROASTED CASHEW SAUCE

1½ cups/210 g raw cashews, toasted (see page 117)

1 cup/240 ml warm water

3 tbsp fresh lemon juice

¼ cup/60 ml extra-virgin olive oil

¼ cup/10 g fresh cilantro

½ tsp ground coriander

¼ tsp cayenne pepper

½ tsp ground cumin

1¼ tsp salt

Pinch of freshly ground black pepper

To make the salad: Combine the cucumbers, tomatoes, parsley, cilantro, onion, lemon juice, oil, ½ tsp salt, and a pinch of pepper in a large bowl and toss to combine. Season with salt and pepper. Set aside, or refrigerate covered, for up to 1 day before serving.

To make the sauce: Combine the cashews, water, the lemon juice, oil, cilantro, coriander, cayenne, cumin, salt, and pepper in a food processor and process until the mixture is smooth and thick, 2 to 3 minutes. Transfer the sauce to a container and set aside, or refrigerate, covered, for up to 3 days before using.

To make the falafel: Position a rack in the lower third of the oven and preheat it to 375° F/190° C/gas 5. Using a pastry brush, generously oil a rimmed baking sheet.

Combine the beans, parsley, onion, cilantro, olive oil, pine nuts, garlic, cumin, salt, coriander, baking soda, black pepper, cayenne, and lemon zest in a food processor. Pulse in short bursts until the mixture is finely chopped, but not pureed, stopping once or twice to scrape down the sides of the bowl. Add the flour to the mixture and pulse until just combined. The mixture should hold together when rolled into a ball and not stick to your fingers.

FALAFEL

3 cups/480 g cooked garbanzo beans (rinsed and drained if canned)

1 cup/30 g packed fresh flat-leaf parsley

½ small yellow onion, coarsely chopped

¼ cup/10 g packed fresh cilantro

2 tbsp extra-virgin olive oil

3 tbsp pine nuts, toasted (see page 117)

4 garlic cloves

2 tsp ground cumin

1 tsp salt

1 tsp ground coriander

½ tsp baking soda

½ tsp freshly ground black pepper

¼ to ½ tsp cayenne pepper

Zest of 1 lemon

⅓ cup/45 g whole-wheat pastry flour

4 whole-wheat pitas

Using a scant ¼ cup/60 g of falafel batter for each, form 16 patties, about ½ in/12 mm thick by 2 in/5 cm wide. Arrange the patties on the prepared baking sheet. Bake for 10 minutes, then gently flip the falafel over and continue baking until they are cooked through and golden brown, about 10 minutes. Remove from the oven and let cool for a few minutes.

Once the falafel are out of the oven, place the pitas directly on the rack and warm them for about 4 minutes.

To assemble the falafel pitas, cut a pita in half and gently open to form a pocket. Fill with ¼ cup/30 g of the salad, two falafel patties, and a generous dollop of the sauce. Repeat with the remaining pita. Serve immediately.

1 SERVING (½ OF A FILLED PITA): CALORIES: 510 | FAT: 30G | CARBS: 53G | PROTEIN: 15G | SODIUM: 1,140MG | DIETARY FIBER: 40% | POTASSIUM: 19% | VITAMIN A: 25% | VITAMIN C: 45% | THIAMIN: 25% | RIBOFLAVIN: 8% | NIACIN: 10% | VITAMIN B₆: 20% | FOLATE: 40% | IRON: 35% | COPPER: 50% | PHOSPHORUS: 35% | MAGNESIUM: 40% | ZINC: 25%

BARLEY, QUINOA, *and* CANNELLINI BEAN LOAF (*or* BURGERS)

My husband calls this my "No Meat Loaf," and he means it as a compliment. We're all more than satisfied eating this loaf packed with healthy variety and nutrients. Barley, quinoa, cannellini beans, pine nuts, chia seeds, onion, garlic, celery, and carrots are delicious together and deliver high protein, fiber, iron, and lots of vitamins and minerals. I use hulled barley versus pearled because of its superior fiber and vitamin content, but pearled is healthy, too, and cooks in less time. This is comfort food at its best when served with our Country Mashed Potatoes and Mushroom Gravy (page 169).

The mixture also makes a great burger topped with a thick slice of ripe tomato. Simply form the mixture into twelve patties, refrigerate at least 2 hours, and then slowly cook the burgers in a large skillet filmed with olive oil, until golden brown on both sides. My favorite way to serve either the loaf or burgers is with sautéed onions and Dijon mustard on the side. This loaf stays fresh for 5 days in the refrigerator and is especially good if you heat the leftover slices in a skillet with a little oil, creating a crispy crust.   —MYRA

Serves 6

3 cups/720 ml Easy Vegetable Stock (page 76) or low-sodium vegetable broth

½ cup/100 g hulled or pearled barley, rinsed

Salt

½ cup/85 g quinoa, thoroughly rinsed

3 tbsp chia seeds (see page 70)

2 tbsp olive oil

1 small yellow onion, small dice

2 medium carrots, small dice

1 stalk celery, small dice

2 large garlic cloves, coarsely chopped

1 tsp dried oregano

Freshly ground black pepper

In a medium saucepan, bring 2½ cups/600 ml of the stock to a boil. Add the barley and ½ tsp salt. Return to a simmer and cook, covered, for 30 minutes (or for just 15 minutes if using pearled barley). Add the quinoa, return to a simmer, and cook covered, for 15 minutes, or until all of the water is absorbed. Remove from the heat, but leave the grains in the pan.

Position a rack in the middle of the oven and preheat it to 350°F/180°C/gas 4. Generously grease a 9-by-5-in/23-by-12-cm loaf pan and set aside.

Mix the chia seeds with the remaining ½ cup/120 ml of the stock and let them sit. The seeds will become thick and gelatinous (this is our egg substitute, which also adds great nutritional benefits).

Meanwhile, heat the oil in a large skillet over medium heat. Add the onion and cook for 4 minutes, stirring occasionally. Add the carrots, celery, and garlic and sauté for 2 minutes. Add the oregano, ¼ tsp salt, and a pinch of pepper. Cook, stirring frequently, until the vegetables are tender, 3 to 5 minutes.

1½ cups/255 g cooked cannellini beans (rinsed and drained if canned)

⅔ cup/80 g dried whole-wheat bread crumbs

¼ cup/30 g pine nuts, lightly toasted (see page 117) and finely chopped

2 tbsp chopped fresh flat-leaf parsley

1 tbsp Dijon mustard

Add the beans to the pan with the grain mixture. Mash the mixture with a potato masher until the beans are partially broken up. Add the sautéed vegetables, bread crumbs, pine nuts, chia seed mixture, parsley, and mustard and stir until well combined. The mixture will be thick like cookie dough and a bit of a challenge to stir. Season with salt and pepper.

Transfer the mixture to the prepared pan, press down and smooth out the mixture, and bake until the top is firm and golden brown, 45 to 55 minutes. Allow the loaf to rest for 15 minutes before cutting it into slices and serving.

1 SERVING: CALORIES: 320 | FAT: 11G | CARBS: 46G | PROTEIN: 10G | SODIUM: 480MG | DIETARY FIBER: 44% | POTASSIUM: 13% | VITAMIN A: 70% | VITAMIN C: 10% | THIAMIN: 50% | RIBOFLAVIN: 15% | NIACIN: 10% | VITAMIN B₆: 10% | FOLATE: 15% | CALCIUM: 10% | IRON: 20% | COPPER: 15% | PHOSPHORUS: 25% | MAGNESIUM: 25% | ZINC: 15%

PORTABELLA MUSHROOM BURGERS

Who doesn't love burgers? Portabella mushroom burgers, to be exact. This recipe takes the portabella to perfection: a thick, juicy mushroom, sandwiched between a whole-grain bun along with sweet grilled onion, fresh tomato, crunchy romaine lettuce, and a spicy avocado spread. I like to cook mine in a cast-iron skillet on the stovetop, but they are also delicious cooked on the grill. Sometimes, when I'm feeling decadent, I'll make double portabella mushroom burgers by stacking two mushrooms for each burger. It's best to plan ahead; the more time the mushrooms and onion get to marinate, the better. If you would prefer to skip a step and avoid grilling the onion, simply serve thin slices of raw red onion—my dad even likes it better this way. Assemble the burger ingredients right before you're ready to eat, for the best presentation. Served with mustard, ketchup, and our Baked Sweet Potato Fries with Creamy Ranch Dip (page 173), dinner is bound to be an epic burger experience. Messiness is expected—so keep plenty of napkins on hand.   —MAREA

Serves 4

MARINADE

⅓ cup/80 ml balsamic vinegar

⅓ cup/80 ml extra-virgin olive oil

1½ tsp minced garlic

1½ tsp agave nectar

½ tsp salt

½ tsp freshly ground black pepper

¼ tsp red pepper flakes

4 portabella mushrooms, slightly larger than the buns, stemmed

1 large red onion, sliced crosswise into four ¼- to ½-in/6- to 12-mm rounds

3 to 5 tbsp high-heat oil, such as safflower, plus more as needed

4 whole-grain hamburger buns

To make the marinade: Whisk together the vinegar, olive oil, garlic, agave, salt, pepper, and red pepper flakes in a small bowl.

Using a sharp knife, make three small slits in the top of each mushroom. Transfer the mushrooms and the onion slices to a rimmed baking sheet and douse them with the marinade. Use a pastry brush to make sure each piece is thoroughly coated, especially the soft undersides of the mushrooms. If the onion rounds come apart, gently place them back together. Allow the onions to marinate for at least 30 minutes, and the mushrooms for at least 1 hour.

Heat a very large skillet, preferably cast iron, over medium-high heat, and film it with a thin layer of high-heat oil. Cook the onion and marinade until the onion is golden brown and caramelized, about 5 minutes. Then flip the slices over very gently (I use two spatulas), and continue cooking for another 5 minutes to brown the other side. It may be necessary to do this in batches, adding more oil to the pan as needed. Don't worry if the onion falls apart; it will taste delicious anyway. Transfer the onion to a paper towel to drain, and set aside at room temperature.

Position a rack in the middle of the oven and preheat it to 350°F/180°C/gas 4.

Using the same skillet, coat the pan with a thin layer of high-heat oil, and place it over medium heat. Cook the mushrooms until they are tender, 5 to 8 minutes on each side. It may be necessary to do this in batches, adding more oil to the pan as needed.

SPICY AVOCADO SPREAD

1 ripe avocado

¼ tsp salt

⅛ tsp red pepper flakes

Ketchup for garnishing (optional)

Mustard for garnishing (optional)

1 large heirloom tomato, sliced crosswise into 4 thick rounds

4 large romaine lettuce leaves, cut in half widthwise

Split the buns and place them on a baking sheet. Toast them in the oven until they are warm and slightly browned, 5 to 10 minutes.

Meanwhile, make the spread: Combine the avocado, salt, and red pepper flakes in a small bowl and mash with a fork or spoon. Set aside at room temperature.

Smear 2 tbsp avocado spread on the top and bottom halves of each bun. Add ketchup and mustard, if using. Place one mushroom on the bottom half of each roll. Top with a slice of onion, a slice of tomato, and two pieces of lettuce. Cover with the top half of each bun. Indulge immediately.

1 BURGER (WITHOUT KETCHUP AND MUSTARD, BUN INCLUDED): CALORIES: 520 | FAT: 39G | CARBS: 43G | PROTEIN: 9G | SODIUM: 660MG | DIETARY FIBER: 40% | POTASSIUM: 31% | VITAMIN A: 30% | VITAMIN C: 30% | VITAMIN E: 25% | THIAMIN: 20% | RIBOFLAVIN: 40% | NIACIN: 35% | VITAMIN B₆: 20% | FOLATE: 25% | IRON: 15% | COPPER: 35% | PHOSPHORUS: 30% | MAGNESIUM: 20% | ZINC: 15%

GRILLED FIG SANDWICHES
with ROASTED PISTACHIO PESTO *and* BALSAMIC CARAMELIZED ONIONS

Wow! Just wow. This sandwich is an unbelievably tasty combination of warm crusty bread, savory pistachio pesto, rich caramelized onion, peppery arugula, and sweet and savory grilled figs. I hope you enjoy this magical meal as much as I do. Although there are multiple components to this recipe, it doesn't take too much time to make. Save it for a day when you're craving something spectacular, and turn an ordinary day into an extraordinary one with your first bite. —MAREA

Serves 4

FIGS

1 tbsp extra-virgin olive oil

1 tbsp balsamic vinegar

¼ tsp salt

¼ tsp freshly ground black pepper

2 cups/255 g fresh Mission figs, stemmed and halved

ROASTED PISTACHIO PESTO

¾ cup/85 g pistachios, toasted (see page 117)

½ cup/15 g packed fresh basil

3 tbsp extra-virgin olive oil or nut oil, such as walnut or pistachio

1 tsp fresh lemon juice

Salt

Freshly ground black pepper

BALSAMIC CARAMELIZED ONION

1 tbsp high-heat oil, such as safflower

1 large red onion, thinly sliced crosswise

2 tbsp balsamic vinegar

2 tsp brown sugar

Salt

Freshly ground black pepper

To make the figs: Whisk together the olive oil, vinegar, salt, and pepper in a medium bowl. Add the figs and toss to thoroughly coat all surfaces. Set aside at room temperature while you prepare the other sandwich ingredients.

To make the pesto: Combine the pistachios, basil, olive oil, lemon juice, ⅛ tsp salt, ¼ tsp pepper, and ¼ cup/60 ml water in a food processor. Process them to a coarse paste. Season with additional salt and pepper. Set aside at room temperature.

To make the onion: Heat the high-heat oil in a medium saucepan over high heat. Add the onion and vinegar and cook for 5 minutes, stirring frequently. Add the sugar and season with salt and pepper. Reduce the heat to medium-low and continue to cook, stirring frequently, until the onion is soft and caramelized, 15 to 20 minutes. Set aside at room temperature.

Position a rack in the middle of the oven and preheat it to 350°F/180°C/gas 4.

Place the baguette pieces cut-side up directly on the oven rack. Toast until golden, about 5 minutes.

continued

1 baguette, preferably whole wheat or multigrain, cut in four equal pieces, each split in half

High-heat oil, such as safflower

1⅓ cups/40 g packed baby arugula

Meanwhile, heat a large grill pan or cast-iron skillet on medium-high heat. Film the bottom of the skillet with a thin layer of high-heat oil. Grill the figs, flat-side down, until they are browned and caramelized, 2 to 4 minutes. If the figs are large, flip them and cook on the skin side for another 2 minutes. Using tongs, carefully transfer the figs to a plate.

To assemble the sandwiches, spread the cut surfaces of each baguette with about 2 tsp of the pesto. Place one-fourth of the onion slices, 2 or 3 figs (or as many as will fit), and ⅓ cup/10 g arugula on each baguette bottom. Cover with the baguette tops and serve immediately.

1 SANDWICH: CALORIES: 660 | FAT: 32G | CARBS: 81G | PROTEIN: 16G | SODIUM: 550MG | DIETARY FIBER: 44% | POTASSIUM: 20% | VITAMIN A: 10% | VITAMIN C: 20% | THIAMIN: 40% | RIBOFLAVIN: 20% | NIACIN: 15% | VITAMIN B$_6$: 30% | FOLATE: 25% | CALCIUM: 30% | IRON: 25% | COPPER: 25% | PHOSPHORUS: 20% | MAGNESIUM: 15%

PLANTAIN TACOS *with* PUREED BLACK BEANS *and* MANGO-LIME SALSA

These tacos make a magnificent and memorable meal, and you'll be more than eager to dig in once you see all the components displayed buffet-style. Slices of golden-brown plantains and mango-lime salsa are the star ingredients. There are few things as tasty as a juicy mango, and we've combined this fruit with sweet red bell peppers, jalapeños for a bit of heat, red onion for color and crunch, and fresh lime juice and zest to brighten the flavors. We like to add creamy avocado and crunchy romaine or cabbage to our tacos, but the beauty of this meal is that everyone can assemble their own favorite combinations. Although this recipe takes a bit of time to prepare, the various condiments can be made a day or two ahead of serving. You can also substitute canned refried black beans for my homemade version if you're short on time. For people with big appetites, serve the tacos with sides of brown rice and black beans.   —MYRA

Serves 6; makes 12 tacos

PUREED BLACK BEANS

¼ cup/60 ml olive oil

1 small yellow onion, diced

2 bay leaves

4 large garlic cloves, finely minced

2 tsp ground cumin

2 tsp dried oregano

1 tsp salt

3⅓ cups/565 g cooked black beans (rinsed and drained if canned)

3 tbsp tomato paste

MANGO-LIME SALSA

1 large ripe mango, peeled, medium dice

1 medium red bell pepper, small dice

Grated zest of ½ lime

3 tbsp fresh lime juice

2½ tbsp finely minced, seeded jalapeno

2 tbsp finely chopped red onion

Pinch of salt

To make the pureed beans: Heat the olive oil in a large skillet or saucepan over medium heat. Add the yellow onion and bay leaves and cook, stirring frequently, until the onion softens, about 8 minutes. Add the garlic, cumin, oregano, and salt and cook, stirring constantly, for 2 minutes. Add the beans, tomato paste, and ½ cup/120 ml water. Cook until the beans are warmed through and the liquid evaporates, 5 to 10 minutes. Discard the bay leaves.

Using an immersion blender or a food processor, puree the mixture until it is almost smooth. Transfer it to a serving bowl and serve at room temperature. The black bean puree can be covered and refrigerated for up to 3 days.

To make the salsa: Combine the mango, bell pepper, lime zest and juice, jalapeño, red onion, and salt in a medium bowl and stir gently to combine. Refrigerate, covered, for at least 30 minutes to allow the flavors to meld. The salsa can be made up to 2 days ahead.

continued

TACOS

2 ripe avocados

2 tbsp fresh lime juice

Pinch of red pepper flakes

Salt

Freshly ground black pepper

High-heat oil, such as safflower

3 large ripe plantains (they should be yellow with brown spots, slightly soft, but not mushy), cut on a slight diagonal into ¼-in/6-mm slices

Twelve 6-in/15-cm corn tortillas

4 cups/280 g thinly sliced romaine hearts or shredded cabbage

1 cup/30 g packed minced fresh cilantro (optional)

To make the tacos: Mash the avocados to a coarse paste in a small bowl with a fork. Stir in the lime juice and red pepper flakes and season with salt and pepper. Set aside at room temperature.

Position a rack in the middle of the oven and preheat it to 300°F/150°C/gas 2.

Place two large skillets (preferably cast iron) over medium-high heat. Ready a plate lined with several layers of paper towels. When the skillets are hot, add enough high-heat oil to coat the bottom of each. When the oil is hot, arrange the plantain slices in a single layer and fry until the undersides are golden brown, about 2 minutes. Flip them over and cook another 1 to 2 minutes, or until golden brown. Transfer the plantains to the paper towel–lined plate to absorb excess oil. Arrange the slices on a platter and serve immediately. Alternatively, you can cook the plantains in batches and keep them warm in the oven for up to 10 minutes.

Place the tortillas directly on the rack in the oven and heat until they are warm, 5 to 8 minutes. Alternatively, you can warm them individually in a skillet on the stovetop. Once the tortillas are warm, keep them covered with a clean kitchen towel.

To serve, arrange the warm tortillas, plantains, mango salsa, bean puree, mashed avocado, romaine, and cilantro (if using) on a table. Let everyone assemble their own taco. Start with a smear of black bean puree, then top with 3 or 4 slices of plantain. Add a dollop of avocado and a dollop of mango salsa, then sprinkle with romaine and cilantro.

2 TACOS (INCLUDES BLACK BEANS, PLANTAINS, AND MANGO SALSA): CALORIES: 580 | FAT: 24G | CARBS: 84G | PROTEIN: 16G | SODIUM: 570MG | DIETARY FIBER: 80% | POTASSIUM: 40% | VITAMIN A: 60% | VITAMIN C: 120% | VITAMIN E: 20% | THIAMIN: 30% | RIBOFLAVIN: 20% | NIACIN: 20% | VITAMIN B$_6$: 35% | FOLATE: 90% | CALCIUM: 20% | IRON: 30% | COPPER: 30% | PHOSPHORUS: 40% | MAGNESIUM: 40% | ZINC: 15%

BUTTERNUT SQUASH, BLACK BEAN, and KALE TAMALES with SPICY TOMATILLO SALSA

I first tried tamales, a traditional dish in certain parts of Latin America, when I traveled to Mexico as a teenager. But it wasn't until I was living in a vegan cooperative house in college that I learned to make them. One Sunday, my friends and I spent the entire day creating tamales to serve sixty people for a communal meal, and since then they are one of my favorite dishes to cook.

Tamales are made from steamed or boiled masa (a starchy corn dough) wrapped around a filling of meats, cheese, or vegetables. This recipe is not as heavy as meat-based tamales, but tempeh and beans provide ample protein. Anyone can help assemble tamales, and the long prep time makes them even more satisfying and special when you finally sit down to eat. If you don't have a whole day to devote to tamale making, you can prepare the masa and the filling up to 3 days ahead. They cook faster and more evenly in two separate steamer pots; borrow an extra pot if you have only one. They also freeze extremely well—so don't worry about making too many. Serve the tamales with my easy Spicy Tomatillo Salsa or your favorite store-bought fresh tomatillo salsa. —MAREA

Serves 8 to 12; makes about 24 tamales

MASA DOUGH

4½ cups/630 g instant corn masa flour (Maseca is a popular brand)

2½ tsp salt

1 tsp baking powder

1 tsp ground cumin

1 tsp garlic powder

1 tsp sweet paprika

2¾ cups/660 ml Easy Vegetable Stock (page 76) or low-sodium vegetable broth

1 cup/240 ml extra-virgin olive oil

2 tbsp fresh lime juice

FILLING

¼ cup/60 ml canola or sunflower oil

½ medium yellow onion, small dice

To make the masa dough: Whisk together the masa flour, salt, baking powder, cumin, garlic powder, and paprika in a medium bowl. Add the stock, olive oil, and lime juice. Mix with clean hands until thoroughly combined. The masa should be about the texture of cookie dough. Set aside if you plan to assemble the tamales within 2 hours, or cover and refrigerate for up to 3 days.

To make the filling: Warm the canola oil in a large skillet over medium-high heat. Add the onion and sauté until it becomes translucent, about 4 minutes. Add the squash and tempeh, stirring frequently to avoid burning, until the squash softens, about 6 minutes. Lower the heat to medium-low and add the kale, beans, cumin, salt, pepper, red pepper flakes, paprika, and cayenne. Sauté until the kale has wilted and is tender, 3 to 4 minutes. Set aside, or let cool and keep it in the refrigerator, covered, for up to 3 days.

When you are ready to assemble the tamales, soak the cornhusks in a very large bowl of warm water, making sure they are completely submerged for at least 5 minutes, or until they are softened. Place a large clean dishtowel on the countertop for soaking up the extra liquid from the cornhusks.

continued

1½ cups/210 g peeled small-dice butternut squash

1½ cups/180 g diced or crumbled tempeh (see page 45)

3 cups/90 g packed stemmed and sliced dino (Tuscan) kale

1⅔ cups/285 g cooked black beans (rinsed and drained if canned)

1 tsp ground cumin

1 tsp salt

½ tsp freshly ground black pepper

½ tsp red pepper flakes

½ tsp sweet paprika

½ tsp cayenne pepper

1 package (about 30) dried cornhusks

Spicy Tomatillo Salsa (facing page)

Take one large husk (see Note, below), shaking off the excess liquid, and place it on the dishtowel with the wide end at the top. Scoop out a scant ¼ cup/60 ml of masa, and spread it down the middle of the husk with your fingertips. The masa should be spread as thinly as possible, about 2½ by 2½ in/6 by 6 cm, in the shape of a circle or square. Make sure to leave at least 1 in/2½ cm of husk uncovered on the top end and at least 2 in/5 cm uncovered on the bottom, narrow end.

Place 3 tbsp of filling in the middle of the masa, closer to the top edge.

Fold one side of the cornhusk over the other, forming a tube around the filling and sealing both sides of the masa together. Fold the bottom edge over the seam where the two sides of the cornhusk overlap. Set aside, folded-side down, and repeat.

To cook the tamales, set a steamer insert into a large pot. Use two steamer pots if possible (the farther apart the tamales are in the pot, the quicker they will cook). Pour hot water into the pot so that it comes up to the bottom of the steamer, but not above.

Line the bottom and sides of the steamer with several of the softened cornhusks. This will prevent water from bubbling up and soaking the tamales as they cook.

Arrange the tamales by standing them up at a slight angle, so that they lean against the side of the pot, with the open ends of the tamales facing up. Cover the pot with a lid (or invert a stainless steel bowl over the pot).

Steam the tamales over medium-low heat for 90 minutes if using two pots, or 2 hours if using one pot, adding more water as needed every 20 or 30 minutes. Be sure to add the water in a manner that does not wet the tamales. Using a knife or cake spatula, push aside the tamales to create a small opening into which you can pour the water. Be careful of the hot steam when you remove the lid. The tamales are cooked when the masa is firm to the touch and does not stick to the cornhusk when opened. Serve them hot with tomatillo salsa.

NOTE: If the cornhusks are too small to spread the masa 2½ in/6 cm wide, you can create a larger one by using two cornhusks. Simply place two husks side by side, overlapping by 1 in/2½ cm.

2 TAMALES (NO SALSA): CALORIES: 480 | FAT: 28G | CARBS: 53G | PROTEIN: 12G | SODIUM: 970MG | DIETARY FIBER: 44% | POTASSIUM: 15% | VITAMIN A: 45% | VITAMIN C: 20% | THIAMIN: 50% | RIBOFLAVIN: 25% | NIACIN: 30% | VITAMIN B$_6$: 15% | FOLATE: 40% | CALCIUM: 15% | IRON: 30% | COPPER: 15% | PHOSPHORUS: 25% | MAGNESIUM: 25% | ZINC: 10%

SPICY TOMATILLO SALSA

This spicy salsa is a perfect pairing for the tamales. The combination of heat from the jalapeño, freshness of the cilantro, tanginess of the lime, and sweetness of the tomatillos adds another dimension of flavor to the tamales. It's spicy, so if you want a slightly milder version, you can use half of the jalapeño. Store-bought tomatillo salsa will work fine, but you'll be surprised how easy and delicious it is to make your own!   —MAREA

Makes about 3 cups/720 ml

1 medium jalapeño

1 lb/455 g fresh tomatillos, papery husks discarded, stemmed and quartered

1½ cups/45 g packed chopped fresh cilantro

½ medium white onion, cut into chunks

1½ tbsp fresh lime juice

4 garlic cloves

1 tsp salt

½ tsp freshly ground black pepper

½ tsp sweet paprika

Using metal tongs, place the jalapeño over an open flame on the stovetop. Turn it frequently, until the skin is charred all the way around, 2 to 4 minutes. Remove from the heat and let cool. Using a clean dishcloth, rub off the charred skin. Cut the jalapeño in half and discard the stem and seeds.

Combine the jalapeño, tomatillos, cilantro, onion, lime juice, garlic, salt, pepper, and paprika in a food processor or blender, and process until smooth. Transfer the salsa to a container, seal, and refrigerate for up to 5 days.

⅓ CUP/75 ML: CALORIES: 25 | FAT: 1G | CARBS: 5G | PROTEIN: 1G | SODIUM: 320MG

Organic Food

Growing food without any synthetic chemicals is a passion our family shares. In our home we enjoy our meals even more knowing our food was produced with respect for nature, in ways that are sustainable for the long-term health of our bodies and this planet.

Intuitively, it makes perfect sense that it can't be healthy for humans to be exposed to the chemicals used to kill weeds, insects, and diseases, and now more and more studies support this position. Most of these agricultural chemicals are deemed "safe" without long-term testing on humans and not in combination with one another. We prefer not to worry about dangerous chemicals when we prepare our food.

12 REASONS WE CHOOSE ORGANIC

1. Organic food has been regulated by the USDA since 2002. Strict guidelines are enforced to assure that organic food was grown without any toxic and persistent insecticides, herbicides, fungicides, or synthetic fertilizers.

2. Choosing organic produce greatly reduces our exposure to pesticide residues, which is especially important for children, whose developing bodies are the most sensitive to chemicals. (To learn which produce items have the biggest pesticide loads, go to the Environmental Working Group's Shopper's Guide to Pesticides in Produce at www.ewg.org.)

3. Organic food is produced without genetically modified ingredients (GMOs) and is never irradiated. Organic regulations prohibit the use of hydrogenated oils, artificial colors, artificial flavorings, artificial sweeteners, and artificial preservatives.

4. We see many products today labeled "all natural," but the term "natural" is open to individual interpretation and is regulated by the USDA only with regard to meats. Products labeled "all natural" can use ingredients that were conventionally grown or genetically modified.

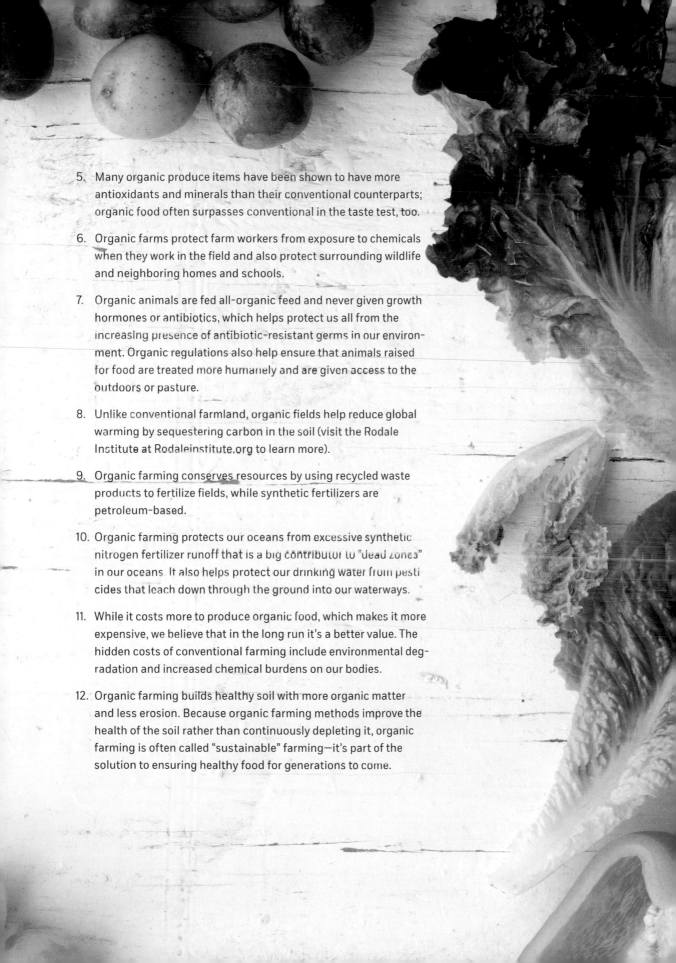

5. Many organic produce items have been shown to have more antioxidants and minerals than their conventional counterparts; organic food often surpasses conventional in the taste test, too.

6. Organic farms protect farm workers from exposure to chemicals when they work in the field and also protect surrounding wildlife and neighboring homes and schools.

7. Organic animals are fed all-organic feed and never given growth hormones or antibiotics, which helps protect us all from the increasing presence of antibiotic-resistant germs in our environment. Organic regulations also help ensure that animals raised for food are treated more humanely and are given access to the outdoors or pasture.

8. Unlike conventional farmland, organic fields help reduce global warming by sequestering carbon in the soil (visit the Rodale Institute at Rodaleinstitute.org to learn more).

9. Organic farming conserves resources by using recycled waste products to fertilize fields, while synthetic fertilizers are petroleum-based.

10. Organic farming protects our oceans from excessive synthetic nitrogen fertilizer runoff that is a big contributor to "dead zones" in our oceans. It also helps protect our drinking water from pesticides that leach down through the ground into our waterways.

11. While it costs more to produce organic food, which makes it more expensive, we believe that in the long run it's a better value. The hidden costs of conventional farming include environmental degradation and increased chemical burdens on our bodies.

12. Organic farming builds healthy soil with more organic matter and less erosion. Because organic farming methods improve the health of the soil rather than continuously depleting it, organic farming is often called "sustainable" farming—it's part of the solution to ensuring healthy food for generations to come.

Chapter 6
SIDE DISHES

POTATO LATKES *with* CHUNKY HOMEMADE APPLESAUCE

You don't have to be Jewish to love latkes—the crispy potato pancakes traditionally served during Hanukkah. And you don't have to wait until the holidays roll around either; my family makes them year-round. Traditionally, latkes include eggs, peeled potatoes, and onions and are served with applesauce and sour cream. I was pleasantly surprised to discover they are still fantastic without any egg, and that I like them even more with the potato peels intact, which means you get all the healthy fiber and nutrients in the peel while you save a time-consuming step. I learned a great trick from Joan Nathan's *Jewish Holiday Cookbook*: Alternating the grating of the potatoes and onions helps keep the potatoes from browning, because the acid in the onions prevents discoloration. I prefer serving latkes as they are being made, but you can keep them warm in a 200°F/95°C oven and serve them all at once. If you aren't inspired to spend the time making homemade applesauce, organic jarred applesauce is what I usually use. But when I have an overflow of apples in my garden, this homemade applesauce is a real treat.   —MYRA

Makes 20 latkes

2½ lbs/1.2 kg russet potatoes (about 6 medium), well scrubbed

1 large yellow onion, peeled

¼ cup/30 g cornstarch

1 tsp salt

Big pinch of white pepper

High-heat oil for frying, such as sunflower or safflower

3 cups/720 ml Chunky Homemade Applesauce (recipe follows) or store-bought

Grate the potatoes and onion, either by hand or by using a food processor with the grating attachment. Alternate grating the potatoes and the onion to help keep the potatoes from browning.

Combine the potatoes and onion in a large bowl and sprinkle them with the cornstarch, salt, and pepper. Mix very thoroughly with your hands and let rest.

Preheat the oven to 200°F/95°C if you plan to use it to keep the latkes warm.

Heat about ¼ in/6 mm of oil in a large 12-in/30.5-cm skillet on medium heat. You can use two skillets if you feel confident watching over more than one pan at a time. Ready a plate lined with several layers of paper towels.

When the oil is thoroughly heated, mix the potato mixture again and drop ⅓ cup/75 ml of the mixture, lightly packed, into the oil and press down with a spatula until it is about ¼ in/6 mm thick. Four latkes should fit in a 12-in/30.5-cm pan. (As you continue to make the latkes, liquid may accumulate in the bottom of the bowl. You can drain this or just avoid it.)

continued

Cook until golden brown, 6 to 8 minutes, and then flip the latkes over and cook the second sides until golden brown, another 4 to 7 minutes.

Remove the latkes from the pan and place them on the paper towel–lined plate. Top the latkes with another two layers of paper towels to absorb excess oil.

Add more oil to the pan if necessary before cooking the next batch. If there are burned pieces of potato in the pan, carefully remove them before adding more latke mixture.

Serve the latkes as they are ready, or keep them warm in the oven while you finish making all the batter.

2 LATKES (NO APPLESAUCE): CALORIES: 150 | FAT: 11G | CARBS: 12G | PROTEIN: 1G | SODIUM: 60MG

CHUNKY HOMEMADE APPLESAUCE

We still live on our original two-and-a-half-acre farm where Earthbound Farm began, and it includes about a dozen apple trees. When apple season arrives, so does my yen for home-made applesauce. It cooks quickly—and is especially yummy with a variety of crisp, flavorful apples. This recipe makes just the right size batch for my latkes. I prefer applesauce still warm from the stove, but my family also appreciates the contrast of cold applesauce with warm latkes. Try it both ways to find out which you like best.

Makes 3 cups/720 ml

6 large apples, peeled, cored, and cut into large dice

Place the apples and 1½ cups/360 ml water in a 10-in-/25-cm-wide, 6-qt/5.7-L pot. Cover, bring the water to a boil, and then lower the heat to a rapid simmer. Simmer, covered for 10 minutes, stirring occasionally.

Remove the lid and continue to cook for about 10 minutes more, stirring regularly, until most of the apples have broken apart and become applesauce, and those that are still intact are tender and easily pierced by a fork. Allow to cool to desired temperature before serving.

½ CUP/120 ML: CALORIES: 60 | FAT: 0G | CARBS: 16G | PROTEIN: 0G | SODIUM: 0MG | DIETARY FIBER: 12%

COUNTRY MASHED POTATOES *with* MUSHROOM GRAVY

It's hard to compete with mashed potatoes and gravy when you're looking for comfort food. These mashed potatoes have a delicious olive oil flavor, and the addition of flat-leaf parsley right before serving adds a bright, fresh note. The rich mushroom gravy is a real treat. I like my mashed potatoes with the skins on—they look more rustic and have more fiber and nutrients. But if you don't like skins in your mashed potatoes, feel free to peel the potatoes before cooking them.   —MYRA

Serves 6

3 lb/1.4 kg yellow potatoes (Yukon Gold or another creamy, flavorful variety), large dice

Salt

½ cup/120 ml plain, unsweetened soymilk

½ cup/15 g packed chopped fresh flat-leaf parsley

¼ cup/60 ml extra-virgin olive oil

Mushroom Gravy (page 170)

Combine the potatoes, 6 cups/1.4 L water, and 1 tsp salt in a 6-qt/5.7-L pot. Bring them to a boil over high heat. Reduce the heat to maintain a simmer, cover, and cook for 15 to 20 minutes, stirring occasionally, until the potatoes are tender when pierced with a fork.

Reserve 1 cup/240 ml of the cooking water, then drain the potatoes. Return the potatoes to the pot. Add the soymilk and ¾ tsp salt. Mash the potatoes with a potato masher until most of the mixture is smooth, leaving as many chunks as you like. If the potatoes are too stiff and dry, add some of the reserved cooking liquid to thin the mixture. Stir in the parsley and oil. Season with additional salt. Serve hot with the mushroom gravy.

1 SERVING (MASHED POTATOES ONLY): CALORIES: 280 | FAT: 9G | CARBS: 41G | PROTEIN: 6G | SODIUM: 700MG | VITAMIN C. 90%

MUSHROOM GRAVY

This mushroom gravy is rich and very flavorful, partially because of the dried porcini mushrooms and their soaking liquid. It pairs perfectly with mashed potatoes, but it's also great with our Barley, Quinoa, and Cannelini Bean Loaf (page 148) and our Whole-Wheat Biscuits (page 141). Notice that the porcini mushrooms need to soak for 30 minutes, so remember to start those early.

Makes about 4 cups/960 ml

½ oz/15 g dried porcini mushrooms

1½ cups/360 ml boiling water

¼ cup plus 3 tbsp/105 ml olive oil

1 small yellow onion, small dice

½ tsp dried thyme

8 oz/225 g cremini or white button mushrooms, rinsed, stemmed, cut in half and thinly sliced

Salt

Freshly ground black pepper

¼ cup/30 g unbleached all-purpose flour

2 cups/480 ml Easy Vegetable Stock (page 76) or low-sodium vegetable broth, heated

In a small bowl, combine the porcini with the boiling water and cover with a plate. Let sit for 30 minutes, or until soft. Drain the mushrooms and reserve the liquid. Chop the mushrooms into small dice. Strain the soaking liquid through a coffee filter and set aside.

In a large skillet, heat 3 tbsp of the oil over medium heat. Add the onion and sauté until it softens, about 4 minutes. Add the thyme and cook for another minute. Add the fresh mushrooms and chopped porcini, ¼ tsp salt, and a pinch of pepper. Cover the skillet and cook until the mushrooms are soft, stirring frequently. Remove the skillet from the heat and keep covered.

Heat the remaining ¼ cup/60 ml of the oil in a medium saucepan over medium heat. Whisk in the flour, reduce the heat to medium-low, and cook, whisking constantly, for 3 minutes. Slowly whisk in the hot stock and the reserved mushroom soaking liquid. Maintain a low simmer and cook the gravy, whisking frequently, until it begins to thicken, about 5 minutes. Add ¾ tsp salt and the mushroom mixture. Simmer uncovered for 5 minutes, stirring often. Season with salt and pepper. Serve hot.

⅔ CUP/165 ML GRAVY: CALORIES: 190 | FAT: 16G | CARBS: 10G | PROTEIN: 3G | SODIUM: 400MG

BAKED SWEET POTATO FRIES *with* CREAMY RANCH DIP

I have always loved sweet potato fries, even more than traditional French fries. Crispy baked sweet potatoes dipped in creamy ranch dip—what could be better? This recipe works best using two baking sheets, because the fries need to be separate from each other to crisp up. In order to get the fries crispy when baked, it's important to soak the raw sweet potato sticks in water before baking—for at least 1 hour, and up to 8 hours. You can make this easy sauce while the fries bake, using Vegenaise or a similar product as the base. It's a perfect recipe to satisfy a hungry crowd.   —MAREA

Serves 4

SWEET POTATO FRIES

1½ lbs/680 g sweet potatoes, peeling optional, cut into ¼- to ⅓-in-/6- to 8-mm-thick sticks

3 tbsp cornstarch

1 tsp salt

½ tsp sweet paprika

¼ tsp freshly ground black pepper

3 tbsp olive oil

CREAMY RANCH DIP

¾ cup/180 ml Vegenaise or similar product

2 tsp finely minced fresh flat-leaf parsley

¾ tsp garlic powder

¾ tsp onion powder

½ tsp apple cider vinegar

½ tsp finely minced fresh dill

¼ tsp freshly ground black pepper

Salt

To make the fries: First, let the sweet potato sticks soak in a large bowl of cold water for at least 1 hour, and up to 8 hours. (Refrigerate, especially if soaking for more than 1 hour.)

Position a rack in the middle of the oven and preheat it to 450°F/230°C/gas 8.

Strain the sweet potatoes in a colander and rinse them.

In a large mixing bowl, combine the cornstarch, salt, paprika, and pepper. Stir to combine.

If the sweet potatoes are still damp at this point, dry them off with a clean kitchen towel. Place the potatoes in the bowl with the cornstarch mixture and toss with your hands until each stick is thoroughly coated with the mixture.

Pour the oil over the sweet potatoes, and toss until thoroughly combined. Spread them on two large baking sheets, as separate from each other as possible. Bake on the middle rack for 15 minutes each.

Flip each fry over with a spatula. Return them to the oven for another 10 to 15 minutes. Remove and flip each fry again. If the fries are not yet crispy enough, return them to the oven for another 5 to 10 minutes, until they are perfectly crispy.

To make the dip: Stir together the Vegenaise, parsley, garlic powder, onion powder, vinegar, dill, and pepper in a small mixing bowl. Season with salt, and serve with hot fries.

1 SERVING (FRIES ONLY): CALORIES: 170 | FAT: 11G | CARBS: 19G | PROTEIN: 1G | SODIUM: 600MG | VITAMIN A: 240%

3 TBSP DIP: CALORIES: 110 | FAT: 11G | CARBS: 4G | PROTEIN: 0G | SODIUM: 450MG

ACORN SQUASH *with* CRISPY MAPLE PUMPKIN SEEDS

This is a simple recipe—cooked acorn squash mashed with a little olive oil and maple syrup and baked with a maple–pumpkin seed topping—but something about the combination is irresistible. This dish is a perfect addition to your Thanksgiving table, and don't be surprised if everyone wants the recipe. And as a bonus, it's very nutritious, so enjoy every bite.   —MYRA

Serves 6

2 medium acorn squash, cut in half lengthwise, seeded

2 tbsp olive oil

2 tbsp pure maple syrup

¾ tsp salt

Pinch of freshly ground black pepper

¾ cup/105 g raw, unsalted pumpkins seeds, lightly toasted (see page 72) and coarsely chopped

Pinch of cayenne pepper

Preheat the oven to 400°F/200°C/gas 6 and lightly grease a large baking dish.

Cook the squash in the baking dish, cut-side down, for about 30 minutes, until the squash is easily pierced with a fork. Let the squash sit for 15 to 20 minutes, until it is cool enough to handle.

Scoop out the squash flesh with a large spoon. In a medium bowl, mash the squash with a potato masher until smooth. Stir in 1 tbsp of the oil, 1 tbsp of the syrup, ½ tsp salt, and the pepper. Spread the mixture evenly in a 9-by-9 in/23-by-23-cm baking pan.

Raise the oven temperature to 425°F/220°C/gas 7.

Make the topping by stirring together the pumpkins seeds, the remaining 1 tbsp of the oil, 1 tbsp of the syrup, and ¼ tsp salt, plus a small pinch of cayenne. Spread the topping evenly over the squash mixture.

Bake for about 20 minutes, or until the topping is golden brown. Serve warm.

1 SERVING: CALORIES: 170 | FAT: 6G | CARBS: 29G | PROTEIN: 3G | SODIUM: 300MG | DIETARY FIBER: 24% | POTASSIUM: 20% | VITAMIN A: 10% | VITAMIN C: 25% | THIAMIN: 15% | VITAMIN B$_6$: 15% | MAGNESIUM: 20%

CUMIN-ROASTED CAULIFLOWER *and* CARROTS

I love alliteration, so it was hard to resist calling this recipe Cauliflower and Carrots Cooked with Cumin, Coriander, and Cayenne. Whatever the title, this is a delicious and simple way to impart great flavor to vegetables. If you take the extra minute to freshly grind cumin and coriander seeds, it tastes even better. This wonderful side dish goes with almost every entree, but I especially like it with our Lentil and Potato Curry (page 135). As a bonus, these vegetables also taste wonderful cold, so save any leftovers to toss in a salad.   —MYRA

Serves 4

1 large head cauliflower, cut into bite-size pieces

2 large carrots, cut into ⅓- to ½-in/8- to 12-mm slices

3 tbsp olive oil

1 tbsp ground cumin (freshly ground if possible)

1 tsp ground coriander (freshly ground if possible)

½ tsp salt

Pinch of cayenne pepper

Preheat the oven to 400°F/200°C/gas 6.

Spread the cauliflower and carrots in a large rimmed roasting pan. Drizzle the oil over them and toss with your hands until they are thoroughly coated.

In a small bowl, blend the cumin, coriander, salt, and cayenne together with a fork. Sprinkle the spices evenly over the vegetables and toss with your hands until the vegetables are evenly coated. Make sure the vegetables are spread out on the pan and not touching each other if possible.

Roast the vegetables for 45 minutes, stirring after 15 minutes, then twice more at 10-minute intervals, making sure they remain spread out on the pan. The vegetables are done when they are firm but easily pierced with a fork and beginning to turn golden brown. If they need more time in the oven after the initial 45 minutes, keep a close eye on them, stirring every 5 minutes. Serve the vegetables warm or at room temperature.

1 SERVING: CALORIES: 160 | FAT: 12G | CARBS: 12G | PROTEIN: 4G | SODIUM: 350MG | DIETARY FIBER: 24% | POTASSIUM: 12% | VITAMIN A: 190% | VITAMIN C: 130% | VITAMIN B₆: 20% | FOLATE: 20% | IRON: 10%

RAINBOW CHARD *with* DRIED APRICOTS *and* PINE NUTS

Dried apricots and chard may seem like an odd combination, but they go together surprisingly well. The dried fruit has a nice sweet-tart bite that complements the chard and caramelized onions. Toasted pine nuts sprinkled on top give it an almost decadent accent. Caramelizing onions takes about a half hour, but if you prep the other ingredients while you are cooking the onions, the timing works out perfectly. Regular Swiss chard works just fine for this recipe, but when beautiful rainbow chard is available, I enjoy its pretty red, yellow, and orange stems.   —MYRA

Serves 4

2 tbsp extra-virgin olive oil

2 medium yellow onions, cut in half and thinly sliced lengthwise

1½ lb/680 g rainbow chard

1½ oz/40 g dried apricots, preferably Turkish, cut crosswise into thin strips about ⅛ in/3 mm wide

Zest of 1 small orange

Salt

Freshly ground black pepper

⅓ cup/40 g pine nuts, toasted (see page 117)

Heat the oil in a large skillet over medium to medium-low heat. Add the onions and cook, stirring occasionally, until the onions are caramelized, 30 to 35 minutes. Transfer them to a bowl and set aside at room temperature. Reserve the skillet for cooking the chard.

Rinse the chard and cut the ribs off the leaves. Cut the ribs crosswise into ¼-in/6-mm-thick slices and set aside. Stack the leaves and cut them crosswise into ½-in/12-mm strips; set aside separately.

Place the chard stems in a large skillet that has a tight-fitting lid. Add ¼ cup/60 ml water. Cover the pan and steam over medium heat until the stems are crisp-tender, about 5 minutes. Add the chard leaves and 2 tbsp water. Cover and cook, stirring occasionally, until the chard is tender and the water has evaporated. If the water evaporates before the chard is tender, add an additional splash of water.

Remove the lid and add the caramelized onions, apricots, and orange zest. Stir to combine, and season with salt and pepper. Serve topped with the pine nuts.

1 SERVING: CALORIES: 260 | FAT: 15G | CARBS: 29G | PROTEIN: 6G | SODIUM: 790MG | DIETARY FIBER: 28% | POTASSIUM: 30% | VITAMIN A: 170% | VITAMIN C: 90% | THIAMIN: 10% | FOLATE: 90% | CALCIUM: 10% | IRON: 20%

BARLEY *with* SPINACH *and* GREEN OLIVES

Although this recipe is a side dish, barley enthusiasts (like me and my two children) will happily eat it by the bowlful. Olives are the surprise ingredient here; their briny bite perfectly complements the sweet, chewy barley and the earthy flavor of baby spinach. Pearled barley, which is high in fiber and a good source of protein, offers a great change of pace from brown rice, and it cooks in the same amount of time. Serve this dish with a soup and salad, and you'll have a delightful and complete meal. If you cook the barley ahead of time, this dish comes together very quickly.   —MYRA

Serves 6

1 cup/200 g pearled barley, rinsed

Salt

4 tbsp extra-virgin olive oil

1 medium yellow onion, medium dice

1 large garlic clove, finely chopped

1 tsp dried oregano

5 oz/140 g baby spinach

½ cup/70 g chopped green salad olives (without pimientos)

Freshly ground black pepper

Place the barley, 2½ cups/600 ml water, and ½ tsp salt in a medium saucepan. Cook on high heat, covered, until it comes to a boil. Reduce the heat to low to maintain a simmer, and cook, covered, until the barley is chewy but tender and all the water is absorbed, 35 to 45 minutes. Remove the pan from the heat, fluff the barley with a fork, and let sit, covered, for 5 to 10 minutes.

Heat 2 tbsp of the oil in a 12-in/30.5-cm skillet (preferably cast iron) over medium heat. Add the onion, and cook, stirring frequently, until it is soft, about 8 minutes. Add the garlic and oregano and cook for 2 minutes.

Stir the barley into the onion mixture and add the remaining 2 tbsp oil, stirring to combine. Heat slowly over medium heat and, when the barley is hot, add the spinach in handfuls, stirring continually. When all the spinach has been added, stir in the olives. Cook until the spinach is just wilted and the olives are warm, 1 to 2 minutes. Remove the skillet from the heat, season with salt and pepper, and serve.

1 SERVING: CALORIES: 230 | FAT: 12G | CARBS: 30G | PROTEIN: 5G | SODIUM: 580MG | DIETARY FIBER: 28% | POTASSIUM: 10% | VITAMIN A: 45% | VITAMIN C: 15% | THIAMIN: 15% | VITAMIN B$_6$: 10% | FOLATE: 15% | IRON: 10% | COPPER: 10% | PHOSPHORUS: 10% | MAGNESIUM: 15%

STEAMED ARTICHOKES *with* DIJON-GARLIC DIPPING SAUCE

Growing up in New York City, I considered artichokes a rare and exotic treat. Now that I'm living in central California where virtually all the artichokes in the United States are grown, they are a staple vegetable. What a fun experience to eat a flower, one petal at a time, dipping each bite into a savory sauce, until you get to the meaty and delicious heart at the center. To eat the heart, scrape out the inedible fuzz (called the "choke") of the cooked artichoke with a knife, and then you can slice the heart into bite-size pieces. When shopping, look for firm and heavy artichokes that are nice and green. You can make this recipe a side dish or appetizer for eight or even sixteen by cutting the artichokes in half or in quarters. They are also delicious served with Creamy Avocado Dressing (page 58), Caesar Dressing (page 61), or Dijon Vinaigrette (page 64). —MYRA

Serves 4

4 large artichokes

DIJON-GARLIC DIPPING SAUCE

1 cup/240 ml Vegenaise or similar product

¼ cup/60 ml olive oil

2 large garlic cloves

2 tbsp Dijon mustard

2 tbsp plus 2 tsp white wine vinegar

2 tbsp chopped fresh flat-leaf parsley

2 tsp prepared horseradish

½ tsp salt

Place a large pot on the stovetop over high heat. Fill it with about 1 in/2.5 cm water, cover, and bring to a boil.

Cut the stem of each artichoke so that only about ¼ in/6 mm remains. Make sure it is flat so it can stand up on its own. Cut about 1 in/2.5 cm off the top of each artichoke and discard. If you'd like, use scissors to cut off the thorny tips of the remaining outer leaves.

Add the artichokes to the pot of boiling water, stem-side down, and cover. Cook on medium heat until the tip of a knife easily pierces the bottom of the artichokes, 35 to 45 minutes (less time if you are cooking small or medium artichokes).

While the artichokes steam, make the sauce: Combine the Vegenaise, oil, garlic, mustard, vinegar, parsley, horseradish, and salt in a food processor with the blade attachment and blend until smooth, scraping down the sides once or twice to make sure all the ingredients are fully incorporated.

Remove the artichokes with tongs and let them cool slightly. Serve warm with small bowls of the sauce on the side.

1 ARTICHOKE WITH ¼ CUP/60 ML SAUCE: CALORIES: 250 | FAT: 19G | CARBS: 16G | PROTEIN: 4G | SODIUM: 580MG | DIETARY FIBER: 44% | POTASSIUM: 11% | VITAMIN C: 20% | FOLATE: 25% | MAGNESIUM: 15%

MISO-ROASTED EGGPLANT

For years, I have been searching for the perfect way to glorify the eggplant—and I finally found it. Through a process of salting, marinating, searing, and then baking, the eggplant becomes amazingly flavorful and perfectly tender. While this sounds time-consuming, it is easy and totally worth it. This recipe works best with Japanese eggplants or other long, thin varieties. But if you can find only the large Italian variety, simply cut it into slices about 1 in/2.5 cm thick. Garnished with fresh basil leaves and toasted sesame seeds and served alongside brown rice or with our Teriyaki Tofu Brocolette on Wild Rice (page 133), this dish is bound to convert many into devout eggplant lovers.   —MAREA

Serves 4 to 6

4 Japanese or Chinese eggplants, halved lengthwise

Salt

MARINADE

3 tbsp white miso

3 tbsp low-sodium soy sauce

2 tbsp toasted sesame oil or olive oil

2 tbsp minced fresh garlic

2 tbsp minced fresh basil

1 tbsp packed brown sugar or agave nectar

½ tsp freshly ground black pepper

High-heat oil for frying, such as safflower

1 tbsp toasted sesame oil (optional)

1 cup/30 g packed julienned fresh basil

2 tbsp sesame seeds, toasted (see page 72)

Spread the eggplants in a single layer on a rimmed baking sheet, cut-side up. Lightly sprinkle with a scant tsp of salt. Set aside at room temperature while you make the marinade.

To make the marinade: Whisk together the miso, soy sauce, sesame oil, garlic, basil, sugar, and pepper in a small bowl. Set aside at room temperature.

Rinse the eggplants with cool water to remove the salt. Pat them dry with a clean kitchen towel. Transfer the eggplants to a rimmed baking sheet, and arrange them in a single layer, cut-side up. Pour or brush the marinade over the cut sides of the eggplants; reserve any unused marinade. Let the eggplants marinate at room temperature for 30 minutes.

Position a rack in the middle of the oven and preheat it to 350°F/ 180°C/gas 4. Line a rimmed baking sheet with aluminum foil.

Film a large skillet (preferably cast iron) with a thin layer of high-heat oil and place the pan over medium-high heat. Sear the eggplants, cut-side down, until they are browned, 2 to 3 minutes. Flip and cook on the other side for 2 minutes. It may be necessary to do this in batches; add more oil as needed. Use a spatter screen if you have one to reduce the dispersal of hot oil during frying. Using tongs, transfer the eggplants to the prepared baking sheet and arrange in a single layer, cut-side up. Brush any reserved marinade over the eggplants and sprinkle with the sesame oil, if using.

Bake the eggplants until they are very tender and can be cut easily with the dull side of a knife, about 20 minutes. Let the eggplants cool slightly, then sprinkle them with the basil and sesame seeds, and serve warm or at room temperature.

2 EGGPLANT HALVES (WITHOUT ADDITIONAL SESAME OIL): CALORIES: 230 | FAT: 10G | CARBS: 33G | PROTEIN: 5G | SODIUM: 1,070MG | DIETARY FIBER: 32% | POTASSIUM: 13% | THIAMIN: 15% | VITAMIN B$_6$: 15% | FOLATE: 10% | IRON: 10% | COPPER: 15% | PHOSPHORUS: 10% | MAGNESIUM: 15%

GARLICKY BRUSSELS SPROUTS *and* CARROTS

This recipe uses fresh garlic two ways—first, whole cloves are sliced and roasted with Brussels sprouts and carrots, then chopped garlic is added to a bread crumb topping for extra flavor. The dish is baked until everything is fragrant, crunchy, and golden brown. I like using young, bunched carrots that are about 8 in/20 cm long, but if you can't find them, substitute mature carrots. This is a satisfying and filling cold-weather side dish that pairs beautifully with soups, stews, and our Barley, Quinoa, and Cannellini Bean Loaf (page 148). —MYRA

Serves 4

8 oz/225 g Brussels sprouts

6 young carrots, cut into bite-size pieces

9 large garlic cloves, cut lengthwise ⅓ in/8 mm thick

2 tbsp extra-virgin olive oil

Salt

Freshly ground black pepper

BREAD CRUMB TOPPING

¼ cup/20 g panko bread crumbs

¼ cup/35 g dried bread crumbs (whole wheat if possible)

2 tbsp chopped garlic

2 tsp dried parsley or basil (or a combination of the two)

Big pinch of salt

Pinch of freshly ground black pepper

2 tbsp extra-virgin olive oil

Position a rack in the middle of the oven and preheat it to 400°F/200°C/gas 6.

Prepare the Brussels sprouts by trimming the ends and cutting smaller ones in half lengthwise, and larger ones in quarters lengthwise. Combine the Brussels sprouts, carrots, and garlic in a 9-by-9-in/23-by-23-cm or 8-by-10-in/20-by-25-cm baking pan. Drizzle with the oil and toss to combine. Season with salt and pepper and toss again. Bake the vegetables for 20 minutes, stirring once.

Meanwhile, make the bread crumb topping: Combine the panko and dried bread crumbs, garlic, parsley, salt, and pepper in a small bowl. Sprinkle the oil over the bread crumb mixture and toss with your hands until well combined. Remove the vegetables from the oven, and press them down into an even single layer. Sprinkle the topping evenly over the vegetables, and press down with a spatula. Continue baking until the topping is golden brown and the vegetables are tender, about 15 minutes more. Serve warm.

1 SERVING (¼ RECIPE): CALORIES: 190 | FAT: 15G | CARBS: 13G | PROTEIN: 3G | SODIUM: 270MG | DIETARY FIBER: 12% | VITAMIN A: 130% | VITAMIN C: 70% | VITAMIN B$_6$: 15% | FOLATE: 10%

EARLY SUMMER SAUTÉ

This dish is so simple, it's almost a surprise to discover how good it tastes: delicate, fragrant, and fresh. Although I prefer eating with the seasons, you can find all these ingredients year-round. I named this Early Summer Sauté because that's the time when these vegetables are best—when asparagus is at its peak and sugar snap peas are just beginning to hang from their vines. It makes an ideal side dish to practically any entree.   —MAREA

Serves 4

2 tbsp extra-virgin olive oil

1 large shallot, thinly sliced

2 cups/230 g fresh sugar snap peas

1 lb/455 g asparagus, ends trimmed, cut into 1-in/2.5-cm pieces

2 medium zucchini, thinly sliced

½ cup/15 g packed fresh basil, cut into thin ribbons

1 tsp fresh lemon juice (optional)

Salt

Freshly ground black pepper

Heat the oil in a large skillet over medium heat. Sauté the shallot, stirring frequently, until it is fragrant and lightly browned, about 4 minutes. Raise the heat to medium-high. Add the peas and asparagus and cook, stirring frequently, for 4 minutes. Add the zucchini and cook until the vegetables are crisp-tender, 4 to 5 minutes more.

Turn off heat and stir in the basil. Add the lemon juice, if using, and season with salt and pepper. Serve immediately.

1 SERVING: CALORIES: 170 | FAT: 8G | CARBS: 21G | PROTEIN: 7G | SODIUM: 170MG | DIETARY FIBER: 24% | POTASSIUM: 29% | VITAMIN A: 100% | VITAMIN C: 70% | THIAMIN: 10% | RIBOFLAVIN: 15% | NIACIN: 10% | VITAMIN B$_6$: 20% | FOLATE: 50% | CALCIUM: 10% | IRON: 20% | PHOSPHORUS: 15% | MAGNESIUM: 15%

Grains

This really could be titled "Whole Grains" since that is such a big theme of this book and an important component of good health. Our recipes exclusively use whole grains because we love their taste and appreciate their better nutrition. When grains are refined, both their bran and germ are removed. The bran is the outer skin of the kernel that contains fiber, B vitamins, and important antioxidants; the germ is the seed's embryo, which contains B vitamins, many minerals, healthy fats, and some protein. According to the Whole Grains Council, removing the bran and the germ removes about 25 percent of a grain's protein, as well as at least seventeen key nutrients. Grains can be ground down into flour or enjoyed in their least-processed form, like wheat berries and rye berries.

Many people are discovering that they have a gluten allergy or sensitivity. While many grains (including all those related to wheat) do contain gluten, there are plenty of delicious gluten-free alternatives. We have noted which grains are gluten-free in the individual grain profiles below. If you need a substitute for wheat in our recipes, most grocery stores now offer gluten-free baking flour blends that closely mimic wheat flour.

BARLEY

Barley is a delicious grain that is chewy and flavorful. One cup/ 200 g of cooked hulled barley contains 7 g protein and 56 percent of your daily value of dietary fiber. You can choose either hulled or pearled barley. We prefer hulled because it is less processed than pearled barley and still contains all of its germ, but pearled barley cooks faster and is still very nutritious.

BUCKWHEAT (GLUTEN-FREE)

Buckwheat is actually a fruit seed related to sorrel and rhubarb, but it functions like a grain. It is a delicious alternative to rice and is a wonderful hot cereal. We love its earthy and nutty flavor. Buckwheat is high in fiber and complex carbohydrates and is also a good source of manganese and magnesium. Buckwheat flour is commonly used in pancakes and crêpes, and it's also used to make soba noodles.

CORN (GLUTEN-FREE)

Corn (also called maize) is one of our favorite foods, and you'll see it featured in many of our recipes, from tortillas to popcorn to delicious corn bread. When you think of all the foods that come from corn—cornmeal (i.e., tortillas chips and polenta), corn flour, cornstarch, corn oil, corn syrup, popcorn, fresh corn (including frozen and canned kernels)—it's no surprise that corn is the largest of all crops grown in the United States. It's interesting to note that more than half of the corn produced in the United States is fed to livestock, and some is even made into ethanol. According to the USDA, 88 percent of the corn grown in 2012 was genetically modified—so make sure to buy organic corn products whenever possible.

MILLET (GLUTEN-FREE)

Millet is actually a tiny seed that functions like grain. Millet contains high amounts of protein and fiber, as well as complex B vitamins, iron, phosphorus, and magnesium. It is very easy to digest and is perfect for cooking, baking, and as a breakfast cereal. In some countries, like India, millet is a staple food; in the United States, many people know it just as an ingredient in bird seed.

OATS (GLUTEN-FREE)

Note that oats are often contaminated with gluten in production, so look for oats marked "Gluten-Free" if you're sensitive to gluten. We use oats in our breakfast cereal, granola, and as a topping for our baked fruit desserts, but they are also delicious in cookies and breads. Whole oats are commonly steamed and flattened to produce the rolled oats we're familiar with. The more they are steamed and flattened, the softer they become and the quicker they cook. We like the chewy texture of "old-fashioned" rolled oats and their thicker cousin, steel-cut oats, but quick-cook oats and instant oats are very convenient. Oatmeal is a good source of dietary fiber, selenium, phosphorus, magnesium, and zinc and an excellent source of manganese. Many health professionals believe oats are helpful in lowering cholesterol levels and preventing cardiovascular disease.

QUINOA (GLUTEN-FREE)

Quinoa is actually a seed (botanically it's related to Swiss chard and beets) but it functions like a grain. Although quinoa is still relatively new to many people, it has been cultivated for more than five thousand years and was known as "the mother grain" by the Incas.

continued

Most quinoa today is grown in the Andes mountains in South America. Quinoa has a delicious and nutty flavor and is very nutritious. In addition to many vitamins and minerals, it is a good source of protein (1 cup/185 g of cooked quinoa has 8 g protein), as well as an excellent source of fiber, manganese, phosphorus, and magnesium. Quinoa is available in red, black, and white varieties. Be sure to thoroughly rinse it before cooking, because quinoa contains a natural plant defense that makes it taste bitter if not removed.

RICE (GLUTEN-FREE)

Rice has been a diet staple in many cultures for centuries and is consumed in huge quantities worldwide. A complex carbohydrate, rice is very nutrient-dense and is higher in protein than most other grains. In this cookbook, we always specify brown rice, because white rice has been stripped of its germ and bran, which removes much of its fiber and nutrients. You can choose to rinse your rice before cooking or not. Rinsed rice will be lighter and fluffier, and unrinsed rice will be denser and chewier because of the extra starch. We generally don't rinse our rice, but we might be in the minority. See how we cook our rice on page 31.

There are many different varieties of rice, including long-grain rice, such as jasmine or basmati; short-grain rice; and wild rice. Wild rice has a chewy, nutty flavor and is actually its own species. It's longer and darker than brown rice and tends to be more expensive.

RYE

Rye is a grain with a rich taste that resembles wheat and has many nutritional benefits. It is a good source of fiber and manganese and has a lower glycemic index than wheat, which makes it a good choice for people with diabetes or insulin sensitivities. Rye is sometimes used in alcohol production and often used for flour. Breads made from rye tend to be denser than wheat breads, with a slightly sour and very rich taste. You can also eat whole rye berries, which are highly nutritious, or rye that has been rolled similar to rolled oats.

WHEAT

There are many types of wheat flour. Durum wheat is typically used for pasta. Wheat for baking is categorized as "hard" or "soft" depending on its protein content, "winter" or "spring" according to what time of the year it's planted, and "red" or "white," determined by the color of its kernels. The two types of flour we use in this book are whole-wheat flour and whole-wheat pastry flour. We truly prefer the taste of whole-grain flour to white, and we like knowing it's healthier. The pastry flour is light enough to substitute for white flour without sacrificing texture.

There are many other grains in the wheat family, including spelt and triticale, all of which contain gluten. There are two other grains from the wheat family we feature in this book:

Farro

Farro is also called emmer wheat. It's an ancient strain that was gradually abandoned for durum wheat and is making a comeback. We use whole farro berries in our Grilled Summer Vegetables and Tofu on Sweet Corn and Farro (page 136), and pasta made with farro flour tops our favorites list.

Bulgur

Bulgur is popular in Middle Eastern, Mediterranean, and Indian cuisines. To make bulgur, wheat kernels are steamed, hulled, dried, and then ground. Because of this processing, bulgur cooks in just 20 minutes. It's a delicious side and can be used in soups, salads, and baked goods.

Chapter 7
DESSERTS

BAKLAVA

Bold and rich, baklava is flaky on top and syrupy on the bottom—the perfect marriage between phyllo dough, nuts, and sweet syrup. You can find phyllo dough that is free of dairy and eggs in most grocery stores in the frozen foods section. Be sure to let it thaw according to the manufacturer's directions before using. The sweet syrup needs at least 4 hours to seep into the nuts and dough. Although the wait is hard, it's well worth it. —MAREA

Makes 24 pieces

FILLING

½ cup/60 g pine nuts, toasted (see page 117)

1 cup/110 g walnuts, toasted (see page 117)

1 cup/120 g pecans, toasted (see page 117)

1 cup/150 g almonds, toasted (see page 117)

2 tbsp agave nectar

1 tsp pure vanilla extract

¼ tsp ground cloves

¼ tsp salt

8¾ oz/250 g phyllo dough, thawed according to manufacturer's directions

1 cup/240 ml Earth Balance or other vegan buttery spread, melted

Preheat the oven to 350°F/180°C/gas 4 and butter a 9-by-13-in/23-by-33-cm baking dish with Earth Balance.

To make the filling: Combine all the nuts, the agave, vanilla, cloves, and salt in a food processor and pulse until the nuts are coarsely and evenly chopped. You can also chop the nuts by hand and combine them with the other ingredients in a medium bowl.

Cut the phyllo dough in half so that it fits in the baking dish, and cover it with a sheet of wax paper followed by a damp kitchen towel to keep it from drying out.

Place one sheet of dough on the bottom of the baking dish. Using a pastry brush, thoroughly coat the dough with melted Earth Balance. Place another sheet of dough on top. Repeat until you have about 8 sheets layered, brushing each one with Earth Balance.

Spread about half of the filling mixture evenly on top of the phyllo dough.

Cover with another sheet of dough, brush with Earth Balance, and repeat until you have about 4 sheets layered on top.

Spread the remaining filling evenly on top of the phyllo dough.

Cover with another sheet of dough, brushing with Earth Balance, and repeat until you have about 8 sheets layered on top. Brush extra Earth Balance on the top layer of phyllo dough.

Using a sharp knife, cut diamond or square shapes in the baklava. You should have about 24 pieces. Make sure you cut all the way to the bottom of the pan.

Bake for 45 to 50 minutes, until the baklava is golden brown and crispy.

SYRUP

1 cup/200 g packed brown sugar

2 tbsp pure maple syrup

2 tbsp agave nectar

2 tbsp fresh orange juice

1 cinnamon stick, broken in half

½ tsp pure vanilla extract

½ tsp orange zest

While the baklava bakes, make the syrup: Combine the sugar, syrup, agave, orange juice, cinnamon, vanilla, and zest in a small saucepan with 2 cups/480 ml water. Bring to a boil, then reduce the heat to simmer and cook for about 15 minutes, until the liquid has reduced slightly. Remove the cinnamon sticks and allow the syrup to cool completely.

As soon as the baklava is out of the oven, pour the syrup over it. Let the baklava sit for at least 4 hours so it can soak up the syrup.

Baklava is best eaten within 3 days of baking, but you can store it in an airtight container for up to 5 days.

1 PIECE: CALORIES: 290 | FAT: 20G | CARBS: 26G | PROTEIN: 4G | SODIUM: 210MG

GINGER, MOLASSES, RAISIN, *and* ALMOND BISCOTTI

Biscotti are crispy Italian-style twice-baked cookies that are especially happy to be dunked in a cup of coffee. This unique recipe yields biscotti with a pretty shade of brown and the rich flavors of ginger and molasses. They are so satisfying that everyone will be surprised to learn they are made without any butter or oil. I got this recipe from Tom Russo, the original owner of the little raspberry farm where Drew and I started Earthbound Farm in 1984. When we arrived, Tom gave us a quick tutorial on caring for the raspberry bushes and introduced us to our first customers. We've stayed in touch for three decades. Tom is now in his mid-eighties, yet I only recently learned that he's a great cook. These are the best biscotti I have ever tasted. —MYRA

Makes about 32 biscotti

2 tbsp chia seeds (see page 70)

¾ cup/150 g sugar

¼ cup/60 ml molasses

1 tsp pure vanilla extract

1 tbsp packed finely diced crystallized ginger

2¼ cups/315 g whole-wheat pastry flour

½ tsp ground cinnamon

½ tsp baking soda

¼ tsp salt

¾ cup/120 g raisins

½ cup/75 g raw, unsalted almonds, chopped

Place a rack in the center of the oven and preheat it to 350°F/180°C/gas 4.

In a large mixing bowl, stir the chia seeds with ⅔ cup/165 ml cold water. Allow to sit for 5 to 10 minutes until the mixture thickens (this is our egg substitute). Whisk in the sugar, molasses, and vanilla. Stir in the ginger.

In a medium bowl, whisk together the flour, cinnamon, baking soda, and salt.

Stir the dry ingredients into the wet ingredients, adding about one-third of the dry mix at a time, and then mix in the raisins and almonds.

In the bowl, divide the dough in half. After moistening your hands to keep the dough from sticking to them, form two 12-in-/30.5-cm-long logs on a parchment-lined baking dish. Press each log down until it's about 1 in/2.5 cm thick at the highest point and about 3 in/7.5 cm wide.

Bake for 30 minutes. Remove the biscotti logs, and reduce the oven temperature to 300°F/150°C/gas 2. Discard the parchment paper, and let the logs cool directly on a rack for 15 minutes.

On a cutting board with a serrated knife, cut the logs into ⅓- to ½-in-/8- to 12-mm-wide slices on a slight diagonal. Put the slices back on the baking sheet, standing up on their flat bottom edge, so that both sides will cook evenly. Make sure to leave at least ¼ in/6 mm between the slices. Bake for 25 to 30 minutes, until the slices are dry and firm. Let the biscotti cool directly on a rack with space in between them. They will continue to crisp and dry as they cool. Any extra cookies should be stored in an airtight container only after they have cooled for a few hours.

1 COOKIE: CALORIES: 80 | FAT: 1G | CARBS: 16G | PROTEIN: 2G | SODIUM: 40MG

COCONUT, ALMOND, *and* RASPBERRY JAM THUMBPRINT COOKIES

These cookies will make you believe in magic because they'll disappear right before your eyes! There are few things I absolutely can't resist, and these cookies are one of them. The combination of coconut, toasted almonds, and raspberry jam is hard to beat. I make them with homemade raspberry jam from our raspberry bushes, which makes them extra special, but any high-quality jam will be almost as delicious. They are wonderful still warm from the oven, but be sure to let them cool for fifteen minutes so you don't burn your mouth on the hot jam. The flavor is best when they've cooled completely.   —MYRA

Makes 15 cookies

1 tbsp ground flaxseed

2 tbsp very hot water (about 180°F/82°C)

½ cup/120 ml melted coconut oil (see page 215)

½ cup/100 g sugar

1 cup/140 g whole wheat pastry flour

¾ tsp baking powder

¼ tsp salt

¼ cup/40 g raw, unsalted almonds, lightly toasted (see page 117) and finely chopped

½ cup/40 g unsweetened shredded coconut

5 tbsp/75 ml raspberry jam

Position a rack in the middle of the oven and preheat it to 325°F/165°C/gas 3. Lightly grease a baking sheet and set aside.

In a large mixing bowl, combine the flaxseed with the hot water. Allow to sit for 5 to 10 minutes until it thickens (this is our egg substitute). Whisk in the oil and sugar.

In a medium bowl, whisk together the flour, baking powder, and salt. Stir the flour mixture into the wet ingredients until just combined, then fold in the nuts and coconut. The mixture will be dry and crumbly but will hold together when squeezed.

Using a tablespoon measure, scoop out 15 slightly heaping tablespoons of dough and roll them into balls. Place the balls on the prepared baking sheet and press down until they are about 2 in/5 cm wide and ⅓ in/8 mm thick, pressing the sides together to keep them from breaking apart. Using your thumbs, press indentations in the center of each cookie that are big enough to hold 1 tsp jam, repairing any big cracks as you go. Fill each indentation with jam.

Bake until the cookies are golden brown, 15 to 20 minutes. Transfer the baking sheet to a wire rack and let the cookies cool for a few minutes before transferring them directly onto the rack to cool completely. The cookies can be stored in an airtight container at room temperature for up to 1 week.

1 COOKIE: CALORIES: 180 | FAT: 12G | CARBS: 18G | PROTEIN: 2G | SODIUM: 50MG

SESAME, ORANGE, *and* HAZELNUT COOKIES

I've always loved sesame candy, so I wanted to create a cookie that featured sesame seeds as a predominant ingredient. These crunchy cookies are packed with sesame seeds, enhanced by the flavors of orange, hazelnuts, cinnamon, and ginger, and adorned by a hazelnut in their center. These cookies aren't too sweet, and sesame seeds are a good source of many minerals and fiber, so they are a relatively healthy choice. If you're serving a Mediterranean meal, like Three-Color Hummus (page 106) and Baked Falafel Pitas (page 146), this would be a perfect dessert.   —MYRA

Makes 30 cookies

2 tbsp ground flaxseed

¼ cup/60 ml very hot water (about 180°F/82°C)

1 cup/200 g packed light brown sugar

½ cup/120 ml melted coconut oil (see page 215)

¼ cup/60 ml pure maple syrup

1 orange, zested

1½ cups/210 g whole-wheat pastry flour

1 cup/140 g sesame seeds

¾ cup/105 g hazelnuts, skins removed (see page 111), 30 whole reserved, the rest chopped medium fine

1 tsp baking powder

½ tsp ground cinnamon

¼ tsp salt

¼ tsp ground ginger

Position a rack in the middle of the oven and preheat it to 325°F/165°C/gas 3. Lightly grease two baking sheets and set aside.

In a large mixing bowl, combine the flaxseed with the hot water. Allow to sit for 5 to 10 minutes until it thickens (this is our egg substitute). Whisk briefly, then whisk in the sugar, oil, syrup, and zest.

In a medium bowl, whisk together the flour, sesame seeds, chopped hazelnuts, baking powder, cinnamon, salt, and ginger. Stir the dry ingredients into the wet ingredients until just combined.

Using a tablespoon, scoop out 30 heaping tablespoons of cookie dough. Roll the dough into balls, then arrange fifteen on each baking sheet, spacing them about 1 in/2.5 cm apart. You should have three rows of five cookies on both sheets. Press down on each ball until the cookie is about ⅓ in/8 mm thick. Place a whole hazelnut in the middle and press down so it's snug.

Bake until the cookies are golden brown, 10 to 15 minutes. Transfer the baking sheets to a wire rack and let the cookies cool for a few minutes before transferring directly to the rack to cool completely. The cookies can be stored in an airtight container at room temperature for up to 2 weeks.

1 COOKIE: CALORIES: 140 | FAT: 8G | CARBS: 15G | PROTEIN: 2G | SODIUM: 25MG

BANANA-COCONUT CAKE

This double-layer cake is shockingly delicious. The cake itself is so moist it melts in your mouth, and between the two layers of scrumptious cake lies a sweet coconut frosting and fresh banana slices. The entire masterpiece, once frosted, is topped with toasted coconut and chopped pecans. Another one of our mother-daughter creative collaborations, this banana-coconut cake is absolutely divine. —MAREA

Serves 12

CAKE

1¼ cups/250 g sugar

½ cup/120 ml melted coconut oil

½ cup/120 ml coconut milk

1¼ cups/185 g mashed ripe banana (3 bananas)

1 tsp pure vanilla extract

2 cups/280 g whole-wheat pastry flour

1 tsp baking soda

1 tsp baking powder

½ tsp salt

½ cup/40 g unsweetened shredded coconut

FROSTING

1½ cups/330 g Earth Balance or other vegan buttery spread, at room temperature

3¾ cups/415 g confectioners' sugar

3 tbsp coconut milk

¾ tsp pure vanilla extract

1 cup/80 g unsweetened shredded coconut

Preheat the oven to 350°F/180°C/gas 4 and grease two 9-in/23-cm springform pans with coconut oil.

In a large mixing bowl, beat the sugar and oil together with an electric mixer or vigorously with a whisk until combined. Add the coconut milk and beat until smooth. Add the bananas and vanilla and mix to combine.

In a medium bowl, sift together the flour, baking soda, baking powder, and salt.

Add the dry ingredients to the wet ingredients. Using a spatula, mix to combine, but avoid overmixing. Mix in the coconut.

Pour half of the batter into each greased pan. Bake on the middle rack of the oven for about 30 minutes, until the edges are brown and a toothpick inserted in the middle of each cake comes out clean.

While the cake bakes, make the frosting: Beat the Earth Balance until fluffy. Stir in the confectioners' sugar, coconut milk, and vanilla and beat until fluffy and combined, about 2 minutes. Stir in the coconut. Refrigerate the frosting while the cake cools.

When the cakes are done, place them on racks and remove the outside edges of each pan. Let the cakes cool completely, for at least 1 hour.

continued

TOPPING

1 cup/80 g unsweetened shredded coconut

2 ripe bananas, sliced into ¼- to ½-in /6- to 12-mm-thick pieces

1 cup/120 g raw, unsalted pecans, lightly toasted (see page 117) and chopped

To make the topping: Place a medium skillet over medium-low heat. Add the coconut and stir continuously with a spatula, until the coconut is golden brown and fragrant. Turn off the heat.

Once the cakes have cooled completely, remove each from its pan and transfer one to a serving plate. Spread some frosting on top of the cake. Place the banana slices evenly on top of the frosting so that the entire cake is covered. Then, gingerly place the other cake on top of the first. Using a rubber spatula, spread more frosting on the top and sides of the cake. Cover it with the toasted coconut followed by the pecans. Cut the cake into 12 slices and serve immediately. If it's a warm day, the frosting will start to soften (so, if not serving immediately, it's best to refrigerate). Store in an airtight container in the refrigerator for up to 5 days.

1 SLICE: CALORIES: 680 | FAT: 53G | CARBS: 52G | PROTEIN: 5G | SODIUM: 450MG | DIETARY FIBER: 28% | POTASSIUM: 13% | VITAMIN A: 20% | THIAMIN: 10% | VITAMIN B$_6$: 15% | PHOSPHORUS: 20% | COPPER: 20% | MAGNESIUM: 20%

VERY CHOCOLATY CHOCOLATE BROWNIES

Chocolate lover alert! These brownies are sensational: very chocolaty, moist, and delectable. It's not only their taste that is rich—they're also rich in healthy ingredients: whole-grain flour, chia seeds, walnuts, coconut oil, and I'll even include antioxidant-packed chocolate on this list. Once baked, you should let the brownies cool at least 30 minutes before cutting into them. At this stage they will be warm and gooey. These brownies taste even better the second day, so they are a great make-ahead dessert. If you plan on serving them on the day they're baked, refrigerate them for an hour or two before serving. —MYRA

Serves 16

8 oz/225 g high-quality semisweet chocolate

½ cup/120 ml melted coconut oil (see page 215)

3 tbsp ground chia seeds (see page 70)

¾ cup/180 ml espresso or strong black coffee (regular or decaffeinated), at room temperature

1¼ cups/250 g packed light brown sugar

1 tsp pure vanilla extract

¾ cup/105 g whole-wheat pastry flour

½ tsp salt

¼ tsp baking soda

⅔ cup/75 g chopped walnuts

Position a rack in the lower third of the oven and preheat it to 350°F/180°C/gas 4. Grease an 8-by-8-in/20-by-20-cm baking pan with coconut oil. Cover the bottom of the pan with a piece of parchment paper, and then grease the top of the parchment paper.

Chop 3 oz/85 g of the chocolate into pieces no larger than chocolate chips. Set them aside. Break the remaining 5 oz/140 g of the chocolate into pieces about ½ in/12 mm wide and put them in the top of a double boiler or in a bowl suspended over a pan of barely simmering water. Stir frequently, until the chocolate is melted and smooth. Remove it from the heat and transfer the chocolate to a large mixing bowl. Stir in the coconut oil, and let cool for 10 to 15 minutes.

Put the chia seeds in a small mixing bowl and whisk in the coffee. Let sit 5 to 10 minutes until it thickens (this is our egg substitute). Whisk again to make sure there are no lumps.

Whisk the sugar into the chocolate mixture. Add the vanilla and the chia mixture and whisk vigorously until blended.

In a medium mixing bowl, whisk together the flour, salt, and baking soda. Stir the flour mixture into the chocolate mixture, then fold in the reserved chopped chocolate and the walnuts. Do not overmix. Transfer the batter to the prepared pan and bake for 40 to 50 minutes, until the top feels dry and the brownies feel firm when a toothpick is inserted in the center. Watch them closely during the final minutes of baking to make sure the edges don't burn.

Transfer the pan to a wire rack to cool. These brownies are best when they cool overnight or are refrigerated for 2 hours after they come to room temperature. When they are ready to serve, cut into 16 squares. The brownies will stay fresh at room temperature for about 5 days in an airtight container, and they also freeze well.

1 SQUARE: CALORIES: 270 | FAT: 15G | CARBS: 34G | PROTEIN: 3G | SODIUM: 100MG | DIETARY FIBER: 8% | COPPER: 10% | MAGNESIUM: 10%

STONE FRUIT CRUMBLE

I am in love with this dessert. It is a perfect way to use any extra stone fruit you have during summer. You'll never again have to waste an overripe peach! I had plums, apricots, and peaches at my house when I created this recipe, but feel free to substitute with nectarines or pluots. You can choose whether or not you want to add blueberries to the recipe, or add another cup of stone fruit. The fruit bubbles with sweetness when cooked and explodes with color and fragrance. Covered with a simple oatmeal topping that turns golden brown in the oven and served with our easy-to-make Creamy Coconut Ice Cream (page 209), this dessert is sure to wow your senses.   —MAREA

Serves 8

FILLING

3 large very ripe plums, medium dice

3 to 4 large very ripe apricots, medium dice

2 large very ripe peaches, medium dice

1 cup/140 g blueberries (optional) or additional stone fruit

¼ cup/50 g packed brown sugar

¼ cup/35 g whole-wheat pastry flour

Big pinch of ground ginger

Pinch of salt

TOPPING

1½ cups/175 g old-fashioned rolled oats

½ cup/70 g whole-wheat pastry flour

⅓ cup/75 ml canola or coconut oil

¼ cup/50 g packed brown sugar

¼ tsp ground cinnamon

Pinch of ground ginger

Big pinch of salt

Preheat the oven to 375°F/190°C/gas 5.

To make the filling: In a 9-by-9-in/23-by-23-cm or 7-by-11-in/17-by-28-cm baking pan, combine the fruit, sugar, flour, ginger, and salt and mix until thoroughly combined.

To make the topping: Combine the oats, flour, oil, sugar, cinnamon, ginger, and salt in a medium mixing bowl and mix until thoroughly combined. Sprinkle over the fruit mixture.

Place the crumble in the oven on top of a baking sheet or aluminum foil to prevent the juices from bubbling over onto the oven floor.

Bake for 40 to 50 minutes, until the top is golden brown and the fruit is bubbly and fragrant. Let cool for 5 to 10 minutes before serving.

1 SERVING: CALORIES: 280 | FAT: 11G | CARBS: 43G | PROTEIN: 5G | SODIUM: 80MG | DIETARY FIBER: 20% | VITAMIN A: 20% | VITAMIN C: 10% | VITAMIN E: 10%

APPLE *and* PEAR MAPLE CRISP

Crispy, crunchy, and easy to make, this sweet and tasty treat features healthy fruit, whole grains, and nuts. This recipe calls for half pecans and half walnuts, but feel free to use just one type or even substitute almonds. The maple syrup in the topping makes it especially crunchy and irresistible. This is a delicious dessert by itself, but for an especially heavenly experience, try it with a scoop of our Creamy Coconut Ice Cream (page 209). While left-overs are delicious, crisps always taste best the day they're made.   —MYRA

Serves 8

4 large apples, peeled and cut into ¼-in/6-mm-thick slices

2 large pears, ripe but firm, peeled and cut into ¼-in-/6-mm-thick slices

1 tbsp fresh lemon juice

CRISP TOPPING

1 cup/115 g old-fashioned rolled oats

⅓ cup/35 g coarsely chopped raw, unsalted walnuts

⅓ cup/40 g coarsely chopped raw, unsalted pecans

¼ cup/35 g whole-wheat pastry flour

2 tsp ground cinnamon

¼ tsp ground ginger

Pinch of ground nutmeg

Pinch of salt

¼ cup/60 ml maple syrup

¼ cup/50 g packed brown sugar

¼ cup/60 ml canola oil

Preheat the oven to 375°F/190°C/gas 5.

In a 9-by-9-in/23-by-23-cm baking dish, combine the apple and pear slices. Sprinkle the lemon juice over the fruit and toss with your hands, and then flatten it so makes an even layer in the pan.

To make the topping: Stir together the oats, walnuts, pecans, flour, cinnamon, ginger, nutmeg, and salt in a medium bowl. Pour the syrup, sugar, and oil over the dry ingredients, and toss with your hands until thoroughly combined.

Spread the topping over the fruit as evenly as possible. Bake for about 40 minutes, until the top is golden brown and crunchy and the fruit feels tender when pierced with a fork. Let cool on a rack for at least 20 minutes. Serve warm or at room temperature.

1 SERVING: CALORIES: 310 | FAT: 15G | CARBS: 45G | PROTEIN: 4G | SODIUM: 45MG | DIETARY FIBER: 24%

POMEGRANATE-ROASTED PEARS

Dessert for breakfast? Absolutely—this unique and tasty dessert is actually healthy enough to start your day. The combination of fruits makes it perfect for winter, when pomegranates are ripe and pears are at their peak. But just as this dish is versatile enough to be served at any meal, it's also versatile enough to be adapted to any season. You can substitute raspberries, blueberries, or sliced strawberries for the pomegranate seeds; also experiment with other rich, sweet juices. Blueberry juice and fresh blueberries make a great combination for spring and summer. And for even more versatility, you can turn this into a sweeter, more decadent dessert by adding a scoop of Creamy Coconut Ice Cream (page 209), or serving it with your favorite vanilla or caramel frozen dessert. The pears get more flavorful after 1 to 3 days in the refrigerator as they steep in their syrup, so this is a great recipe to make ahead of time. —MYRA

Serves 4 to 8

1 qt/960 ml pomegranate juice

3 cinnamon sticks (3 in/
7.5 cm long)

4 whole cloves

1 whole star anise

1 tbsp molasses

4 pears, ripe but still firm, peeled and cut into quarters lengthwise

½ cup/75 g pomegranate seeds

Combine the juice, cinnamon sticks, cloves, and star anise in a medium saucepan and bring to a simmer over high heat. Lower the heat to maintain a simmer, stir in the molasses, and cook with the lid slightly ajar for 20 minutes, stirring occasionally.

Position a rack in the middle of the oven and preheat it to 400°F/200°C/gas 6.

Put the pears cut-side down in a 3-qt/2.8-L (9-by-13-in/23-by-33-cm) baking dish. Pour the hot juice mixture over the pears, making sure all the spices are submerged. Bake for 10 minutes. Using a spoon or slotted spatula, flip the pears over and bake for 10 minutes more.

Raise the heat to 450°F/230°C/gas 8. Flip the pears over again and cook for 10 minutes. Flip the pears a final time and cook until they are just tender when pierced with the tip of a knife, 5 to 10 minutes more.

Remove the baking dish from the oven and let the pears cool in the pan for at least 20 minutes, turning them or basting them with the juice every few minutes.

Transfer the pomegranate juice and spices to a small saucepan. Cook uncovered over medium heat, stirring occasionally, until the mixture is syrupy and has reduced by half, about 20 minutes. Pour the syrup over the pears to enhance their flavor.

Divide the pears among shallow bowls and top each serving with some of the syrup. Serve warm, cold, or at room temperature, sprinkled with pomegranate seeds.

2 PEAR HALVES WITH ¼ OF THE SYRUP: CALORIES: 370 | FAT: 2.5G | CARBS: 94G | PROTEIN: 4G | SODIUM: 55MG | DIETARY FIBER: 60% | POTASSIUM: 17% | VITAMIN C: 30% | VITAMIN B₆: 10% | CALCIUM: 20% | IRON: 20% | COPPER: 15% | MAGNESIUM: 15%

BROWN RICE PUDDING

When I was pregnant with Marea, I craved rice pudding and ate it often, so it feels fitting to include it in our first collaborative cookbook. This version uses brown rice, and it's spiced with cardamom, the primary flavor in *kulfi*, an Indian frozen dessert that was my favorite when I lived in India for a semester during college. If you have time to freshly grind the cardamom, the pudding will be extra flavorful and delicious. Kulfi incorporates pistachios, so I've included them as a topping, and I think they make a perfect complement. Strawberries add color and a fresh flavor, so definitely try adding them if they are in season. Store any leftover pudding in the refrigerator, and heat it in the microwave until it's slightly warm before serving.   —MYRA

Serves 6

1 cup/200 g short- or long-grain brown rice

¼ tsp salt

3 cups/720 ml plain, unsweetened soymilk

⅓ cup/65 g sugar

1 tsp ground cardamom (freshly ground if possible)

1 tsp pure vanilla extract

½ tsp ground cinnamon

½ cup/75 g dates, coarsely chopped

½ cup/55 g pistachio nuts, lightly toasted (see page 117) and coarsely chopped

2 cups/260 g strawberries, sliced into thin strips (optional)

Combine the rice, 2 cups/480 ml water, and the salt in a medium saucepan over high heat. Cover, bring to a boil, and then reduce the heat to low. Simmer, covered, for 30 minutes.

Stir in the soymilk, sugar, cardamom, vanilla, and cinnamon. Return to a gentle simmer and cook, covered, for 10 minutes, stirring occasionally. Add the dates and simmer, covered, for 10 minutes, stirring regularly. If there is still liquid in the pot, continue to simmer uncovered, stirring frequently, until the texture of the pudding is creamy.

Cover and remove from the heat. Allow to sit for 5 to 10 minutes.

Serve warm or at room temperature, topped with the pistachios and strawberries (if using).

1 SERVING (WITH 1½ TBSP PISTACHIOS AND ⅓ CUP/60 G STRAWBERRIES): CALORIES: 320 | FAT: 8G | CARBS: 56G | PROTEIN: 10G | SODIUM: 115MG | DIETARY FIBER: 24% | POTASSIUM: 12% | VITAMIN C: 50% | COPPER: 10%

BLACKBERRY-MINT SORBET

With a rich dark-purple color and explosive flavors, this blackberry-mint sorbet is an amazing adventure for your taste buds. Minty freshness gives way to an explosion of tart and sweet blackberries, culminating with the perfect tang of fresh orange juice and zest. Directly out of the ice cream maker, the sorbet has more of a soft-serve texture. If you want a harder texture, transfer the sorbet to a container and place it in the freezer until firm, about 2 hours. If freezing for more than 12 hours, allow the sorbet to sit at room temperature for 5 to 10 minutes before serving.   —MAREA

Serves 4; makes 1 pint/480 ml

⅓ cup/65 g packed light brown sugar

4 cups/520 g fresh blackberries

¼ cup/60 ml fresh orange juice

¼ cup/10 g packed fresh spearmint

¼ tsp grated orange zest

Pinch of salt

4 sprigs fresh spearmint for garnishing (optional)

Combine the sugar and ¾ cup/180 ml water in a small saucepan over medium heat and cook, stirring frequently, until the sugar completely dissolves. Transfer the syrup to a blender. Add the blackberries and process until smooth.

Pour the blackberry puree into a fine-mesh sieve set over a large bowl. Using a spoon or rubber spatula, work the puree through the sieve until all that remains are the seeds. Discard the seeds and return the puree to the blender.

Add the juice, mint, zest, and salt and process until smooth. Transfer the mixture to the refrigerator and allow it to chill completely, about 2 hours.

Freeze the puree in an ice cream maker according to the manufacturer's directions. If you desire a firmer texture, transfer the sorbet to a container and place it in the freezer for 2 hours.

Scoop the sorbet into small bowls or pretty glasses and garnish with the mint sprigs (if using) to serve.

½ CUP/120 ML: CALORIES: 140 | FAT: 1G | CARBS: 34G | PROTEIN: 2G | SODIUM: 150MG | DIETARY FIBER: 32% | VITAMIN A: 10% | VITAMIN C: 70% | FOLATE: 10% | COPPER: 15%

PEACH-BASIL-LIME SORBET

This sorbet is divine. It's so easy to make, and yet each bite brings with it a complexity of flavor that leaves my head spinning (in a good way). This is a perfect dessert for the heat of summer, when peaches are at their peak and you want something sweet, cold, and refreshing. Directly out of the ice cream maker, the sorbet has more of a soft-serve texture. If you want a harder texture, transfer the sorbet to a container and place it in the freezer until firm, about 2 hours. If freezing for more than 12 hours, allow the sorbet to sit at room temperature for 5 to 10 minutes before serving.   —MAREA

Serves 4; makes 3 cups/720 ml

1¼ lb/570 g ripe peaches, peeled and coarsely chopped

¾ cup/180 ml ice water

¼ cup/60 ml agave nectar

¼ tsp grated lime zest

2 tbsp fresh lime juice

2 tbsp pure maple syrup

1½ tbsp packed minced fresh basil

Pinch of salt

Combine the peaches, water, agave, zest and juice, maple syrup, basil, and salt in a blender and puree until very smooth. Chill the mixture completely before proceeding with the recipe, about 2 hours.

Freeze the puree in an ice cream maker according to the manufacturer's directions. If you desire a firmer texture, transfer the sorbet to a container and place it in the freezer for about 2 hours.

Scoop the sorbet into small bowls or pretty glasses to serve.

¾ CUP/180 ML: CALORIES: 140 | FAT: 0G | CARBS: 36G | PROTEIN: 1G | SODIUM: 150MG | VITAMIN A: 10% | VITAMIN C: 290%

CREAMY COCONUT ICE CREAM

This nondairy frozen dessert (pictured at the back of the photo on page 210) is delicious and unbelievably fast and easy to make. Simply combine the ingredients, place them in your ice cream maker, and voilà!—homemade coconut "ice cream" in less than 20 minutes. Eat it on its own as a wonderfully rich and refreshing treat, or serve it with one of our desserts, like the Stone Fruit Crumble (page 203) or our Very Chocolaty Chocolate Brownies (page 200). This recipe is a great base to use to create new and exciting flavors (see banana variation).   —MYRA

Serves 4; makes 2 cups/480 ml

One 13.5-oz/385-g can coconut milk

¼ cup/60 ml agave nectar

¼ tsp pure vanilla extract

Pinch of salt

In a medium bowl, whisk the coconut milk, agave, vanilla, and salt together.

Freeze in an ice cream maker according to the manufacturer's directions. If you want a firmer texture, transfer the ice cream to a container and place it in the freezer until firm, about 2 hours.

Scoop into small bowls or pretty glasses to serve.

½ CUP/120 ML: CALORIES: 260 | FAT: 21G | CARBS: 18G | PROTEIN: 2G | SODIUM: 130MG | IRON: 20% | COPPER: 10% | MAGNESIUM: 10%

Variation: BANANA ICE CREAM

Add 1 cup/240 ml well-mashed, very ripe banana to the coconut mixture and freeze in an ice cream maker according to the manufacturer's directions.

Serve topped with toasted shredded coconut, semisweet chocolate shavings, and toasted walnut pieces.

MINT–CHOCOLATE CHIP ICE CREAM

Yum! This mint–chocolate chip ice cream (pictured at the front of the photo on the facing page) is amazingly delicious. With fresh bits of mint and the perfect amount of peppermint (not to mention bittersweet chocolate chunks), this ice cream is bound to put an extra spring in your step. For the minty flavor, you can use either peppermint oil or peppermint extract; the only difference is that peppermint oil is four times stronger than the extract, so make sure you know which one you're using. If you want a lower-fat and -calorie option, you can substitute lite coconut milk. The ice cream will taste lighter but still delicious. —MAREA

Serves 4; makes 2 cups/480 ml

One 13.5-oz/385-g can coconut milk

¼ cup/60 ml agave nectar

2 tbsp finely minced fresh mint

½ tsp pure vanilla extract

¼ tsp peppermint extract, or 4 drops peppermint oil

Big pinch of salt

2 oz/55 g finely chopped bittersweet chocolate

In a medium mixing bowl, whisk together the coconut milk, agave, mint, vanilla, peppermint extract, and salt.

Freeze in an ice cream maker according to the manufacturer's directions. After the mixture begins to thicken (about 5 minutes in my machine), add the chocolate and finish freezing. The ice cream will have a soft-serve consistency directly out of the ice cream maker. If you want a firmer texture, transfer the ice cream to a container and place it in the freezer until firm, 2 to 4 hours.

Scoop into small bowls or pretty glasses to serve.

½ CUP/120 ML (WITH REGULAR COCONUT MILK): CALORIES: 350 | FAT: 27G | CARBS: 28G | PROTEIN: 4G | SODIUM: 170MG | DIETARY FIBER: 16% | VITAMIN A: 35% | IRON: 20% | COPPER: 10% | MAGNESIUM: 10%

½ CUP/120 ML (WITH LITE COCONUT MILK): CALORIES: 220 | FAT: 13G | CARBS: 28G | PROTEIN: 2G | SODIUM: 170MG | VITAMIN A: 35%

DOUBLE CHOCOLATE–COCONUT ICE CREAM

This ice cream (pictured on the center left of the photo on page 210) proves that vegan food can be decadent and satisfy all your chocolate cravings. Coconut milk is the base for this very chocolaty ice cream that features shredded coconut, small slivers of semisweet chocolate, and a rich gelato-like texture. The ice cream mixture will need to cool in the refrigerator for at least 2 hours, so plan accordingly. If you want a lower-fat and -calorie option, you can substitute lite coconut milk. The ice cream will taste lighter but still delicious. —MYRA

Serves 5; makes 2½ cups/600 ml

One 13.5-oz/385-g can coconut milk

½ cup/100 g sugar

¼ cup/25 g unsweetened cocoa powder

¼ cup/40 g semisweet chocolate chips or finely chopped semisweet baking chocolate

½ tsp pure vanilla extract

Pinch of salt

½ cup/40 g shredded unsweetened coconut

⅓ cup/50 g thick semisweet chocolate shavings (or thin slivers), none more than ⅓ in/ 8 mm long

In a medium saucepan over medium heat, whisk together the coconut milk, sugar, cocoa powder, chocolate, vanilla, and salt until well combined. Bring them to a light simmer and cook for 5 minutes, stirring regularly. Transfer the mixture to a large bowl and refrigerate until cold, at least 2 hours (stirring periodically speeds up cooling).

When the mixture is cold, stir in the coconut. Freeze in an ice cream maker according to the manufacturer's directions. After the mixture begins to thicken (about 5 minutes in my machine), add the chocolate shavings and finish freezing. The ice cream will have a soft-serve consistency directly out of the ice cream maker. If you want a firmer texture, transfer the ice cream to a container and place it in the freezer until firm, 2 to 4 hours.

Scoop into small bowls or pretty glasses to serve.

½ CUP/60 ML (WITH REGULAR COCONUT MILK): CALORIES: 380 | FAT: 27G | CARBS: 39G | PROTEIN: 4G | SODIUM: 130MG | DIETARY FIBER: 20% | COPPER: 25% | MAGNESIUM: 20%

½ CUP/60 ML (WITH LITE COCONUT MILK): CALORIES: 290 | FAT: 16G | CARBS: 39G | PROTEIN: 2G | SODIUM: 130MG | DIETARY FIBER: 16% | COPPER: 20% | MAGNESIUM: 15%

DECADENT SPICY HOT CHOCOLATE

This recipe is for chocolate lovers only. I laughed out loud the first time I tasted it. I couldn't believe I had created something this decadent! Oat milk makes a perfect base for this rich and spicy hot chocolate indulgence, and the ground ginger, cayenne pepper, and cinnamon stick add a whole other dimension of exciting flavor to this drinkable dessert. If you truly love spicy chocolate, feel free to bump up the cayenne pepper. And if ginger is your favorite spice, add more! Everybody's taste buds are different, so season to taste for your perfect version of spicy hot chocolate. The serving size is small (½ cup/120 ml), so savor every sip. You can also make this recipe into chocolate pudding by adding chia seeds to thicken it (see below). I love it, and so does my mom, but not everyone is thrilled with the crunch of chia seeds in their pudding. Give it a try if you're feeling adventurous.   —MAREA

Serves 8

1 qt/960 ml plain, unsweetened oat milk

5¾ oz/160 g semisweet dark chocolate, small dice

One 3-in/7.5-cm cinnamon stick

¼ tsp ground ginger

Big pinch of cayenne pepper

A few drops of pure vanilla extract

Agave or sugar, as needed

In a heavy-bottomed saucepan, heat the oat milk over medium-low heat.

Once it is warm, add the chocolate, cinnamon, ginger, and cayenne. Cook, whisking frequently, until the chocolate has melted and the liquid is hot.

Remove the pan from the heat and add a few drops of vanilla and agave or sugar, if needed. Serve warm.

¼ CUP/120 ML (NO ADDED SWEETENER): CALORIES: 150 | FAT: 6G | CARBS: 25G | PROTEIN: 2G | SODIUM: 10MG

Variation: CHOCOLATE-CHIA PUDDING

Serves 2

In a soup bowl, whisk 2 tbsp chia seeds with 1 cup/240 ml Decadent Spicy Hot Chocolate. Add 1 tsp sugar and a few more drops of vanilla extract, and whisk again. Cover, and let sit in the refrigerator until it thickens, 10 to 20 minutes.

Coconut

The coconut palm has often been called "the tree of life," because these trees produce food, drink, fuel, fiber, utensils, musical instruments, and so much more. There is even coconut sugar made from the sap of the coconut palm's flowers. Coconut is especially appreciated in vegan cooking because of its buttery oil and rich and flavorful meat and milk. A nutritional powerhouse, coconut is rich in fiber, vitamins, minerals, and healthy fats. Although coconut has not traditionally been part of the American diet, it has been a staple food for many Asian, Pacific Island, Indian, and South American cultures for centuries, and coconut products are currently gaining tremendous popularity in the United States. We *love* using coconut products in our recipes.

SHREDDED OR SLIVERED COCONUT

Shredded or slivered coconut comes from the dried meat of mature coconuts. Coconut meat is a good source of fiber, as well as healthy nutrients like manganese, potassium, and copper. Shredded or slivered coconut is a wonderful ingredient in baking, and you can find it in the baking section of any major grocery store. We always choose unsweetened rather than sweetened coconut, since you can always add sugar, but you can't take it away. Once opened, dried coconut meat will last for about 6 months in the pantry and up to 1 year in the freezer. Try our Coconut, Almond, and Raspberry Jam Thumbprint Cookies (page 195) for a delicious, coconut-y treat.

COCONUT WATER

Coconut water is harvested from young coconuts, which contain more water and softer meat than their mature counterparts. Since young coconuts do not have much meat, the majority of the coconut's healthy nutrients can be found in its water, making it a highly nutritious beverage. Most coconut water that is available in the United States is imported from Thailand, the Philippines, or Brazil and is usually available in the refrigerated drink section of the grocery store. It's delicious and refreshing, packed with electrolytes and other vitamins and minerals. Drinking coconut water is a healthy way to boost your energy, hydrate your body, and add more spring to your step. We feature it in our Tropical Green Smoothie (page 40).

COCONUT MILK

Coconut milk is the thick liquid expressed from the meat of the mature coconut, combined with water. Coconut milk is not to be confused with coconut cream, which is similar but has a higher meat-to-water ratio than coconut milk. Coconut milk is naturally high in fat, making it an ideal ingredient for baking or for coffee drinks. You can find canned coconut milk in most major grocery stores, and often there are both full-fat and low-fat options. It's important to shake the can vigorously before opening, since the milk can separate. Coconut milk is a wonderful, creamy ingredient that we use in our sauces, soups, and desserts, like our Creamy Coconut Ice Cream (page 209).

COCONUT OIL

Coconut oil is extracted from coconut meat. We like to use extra-virgin coconut oil, which is not refined, so it maintains all its good nutrients. Coconut oil is an extremely healthy oil because it is readily absorbed into the body, requiring less digestion than other fats, and its acid profile contains immune-supporting nutrients like lauric acid. Coconut oil is great for stir-frying (on medium or medium-high heat) and for baking—try Myra's Beloved Oatcakes (page 38) or our Very Chocolaty Chocolate Brownies (page 200).

Melting Coconut Oil

It's difficult to get an accurate fluid cup measurement when the oil is in its solid form, and coconut oil stays hard at temperatures below 76°F/24°C, so we generally melt the entire jarful and then measure out the oil. Any unused oil will slowly resolidify, and it's perfectly fine to melt the oil many times. If you need only a small amount of oil, you can use either of the methods below until it seems like there is enough melted oil for your recipe, without having to wait for the entire jar to liquefy.

On the stovetop: Place the entire jar of hard coconut oil (with the lid screwed on tightly) in a small saucepan of water over medium-low heat. If the water begins to boil, you can turn off the heat and the coconut oil will continue to melt. As soon as the oil liquefies, remove it from the water, dry off the jar, and measure out the quantity you need.

In the microwave: Remove the lid and then place the entire jar of coconut oil in the microwave. Heat on high in 30-second intervals until the coconut oil melts.

APPENDICES

THEME MENUS

MIDDLE EASTERN SPREAD
Three-Color Hummus with Garlic–Whole Wheat Pita Chips (page 106)

Quinoa Tabbouleh (page 68)

Baked Falafel Pitas with Chopped Greek Salad and Roasted Cashew Sauce (page 146)

Sesame, Orange, and Hazelnut Cookies (page 193)

ITALIAN INSPIRATION
Mixed Chicory Salad with Avocado, Garlic Croutons, and Pine Nuts (page 56)

Pasta with Creamy Mushroom Sauce (page 127)

Rainbow Chard with Dried Apricots and Pine Nuts (page 177)

Ginger, Molasses, Raisin, and Almond Biscotti (page 196)

ASIAN FLAVORS
Red Leaf, Orange, and Jicama Salad with a Citrus-Soy Vinaigrette (page 55)

Thai Coconut Soup (page 88)

Teriyaki Tofu Broccolette on Wild Rice (page 133)

Brown Rice Pudding (page 206)

SOUTH OF THE BORDER
Colorful Garden Cobb Salad with Creamy Avocado Dressing (page 58)

Butternut Squash, Black Bean, and Kale Tamales with Spicy Tomatillo Salsa (page 158)

Banana-Coconut Cake (page 203)

VEGAN VALENTINE
Raspberry Salad with Baby Greens and Raspberry–Golden Balsamic Vinaigrette (page 50)

Hearty Beet Soup (page 87)

Seared Polenta with Spicy Heirloom Tomato Sauce (page 123)

Double Chocolate–Coconut Ice Cream (page 212)

SUPER HEALTHY SUPER BOWL
Baked Sweet Potato Fries with Creamy Ranch Dip (page 173)

Cabbage and Carrot Crunch Salad (page 63)

Crispy Baked Kale Chips (page 109)

Camille and Marea's Favorite Popcorn (page 114)

Chipotle-Lime Brazil Nuts (page 113)

Four Bean and Sweet Potato Chili with Skillet Corn Bread (page 142)

Coconut, Almond, and Raspberry Jam Thumbprint Cookies (page 195)

ISLAND ADVENTURE
Grilled Hearts of Palm Salad with Grapefruit and Avocado (page 48)

Plantain Tacos with Pureed Black Beans and Mango-Lime Salsa (page 155)

Creamy Coconut Ice Cream (or banana variation; page 209)

CALIFORNIA SPA DAY
Tropical Green Smoothie (page 40)

Spicy Cucumber-Ginger Gazpacho (page 89)

Healthy Greens with Carrot and Parsley (page 65)

Grilled Summer Vegetables and Tofu on Sweet Corn and Farro (page 136)

Pomegranate-Roasted Pears (page 205)

BODY-BUILDING DAY (TOTAL 96 G PROTEIN; 3,070 CALORIES)
Sweet Simmered Cinnamon-Orange Tofu and Brown Rice (page 30; 13 g protein, 400 calories)

Peanut Butter–Banana Smoothie (page 41; 17 g protein, 370 calories)

Colorful Garden Cobb Salad with Creamy Avocado Dressing (page 58; 18 g protein, 620 calories)

Curried Yellow Split Pea Soup (page 82; 23 g protein, 430 calories)

Grilled Summer Vegetables and Tofu on Sweet Corn and Farro (page 136; 22 g protein, 540 calories)

Blueberry Cornmeal Pancakes, 3 pancakes (page 27; 710 calories, 15 g protein)

VEGAN THANKSGIVING FEAST
Spinach Salad with Maple-Roasted Butternut Squash and Walnuts (page 54)

Barley, Quinoa, and Cannellini Bean Loaf (page 148)

Country Mashed Potatoes with Mushroom Gravy (page 169)

Acorn Squash with Crispy Maple Pumpkin Seeds (page 175)

Garlicky Brussels Sprouts and Carrots (page 181)

Apple and Pear Maple Crisp (page 192)

Creamy Coconut Ice Cream (page 209)

KID FRIENDLY
Baked Sweet Potato Fries with Creamy Ranch Dip (page 173)

Eccentric Caesar Salad (page 61)

Seared Polenta Cakes with Spicy Heirloom Tomato Sauce (page 123)

Very Chocolaty Chocolate Brownies (page 200)

CONVERSION CHART FOR COMMON INGREDIENTS

INGREDIENT	APPROXIMATE YIELD
Bell pepper (medium), diced	1½ cups/170 g
Carrot (large), thinly sliced	¾ cup/90 g
Carrot (medium), coarsely grated	½ cup/50 g
Celery, 1 (large) stalk, thinly sliced	⅓ cup/40 g
Cucumber (large), diced	2 cups/270 g
Leek (large), white part only, thinly sliced	½ cup/50 g
Red onion (medium), diced	1½ cups/150 g
Yellow onion (small), diced	1 cup/100 g
Yellow onion (medium), diced	1½ cups/150 g
Yellow onion (large), diced	2 cups /200 g
Parsnip (medium), diced	¾ cup/100 g
Tomato (large), diced	1¼ cups/210 g
Zucchini (medium), diced	1 cup/130 g

CUTTING METHODS

Large dice Large cubes measuring about ¾ in/2 cm on all sides

Medium dice Medium cubes measuring about ½ in/12 mm on all sides

Small dice Tiny cubes measuring about ¼ in/6 mm on all sides

Fine dice Very tiny cubes measuring about ⅛ in/3 mm or smaller on all sides

Mince Very, very tiny cubes, measuring about 1/16 in/22 mm or smaller on all sides

Thinly sliced Pieces about ¼ in/6 mm thick

Julienne Usually ⅛ by ⅛ in/3 by 3 mm and 1 to 2 in/2.5 to 5 cm long

Coarsely chopped Pieces roughly the size of a medium dice

Finely chopped Pieces roughly the size of a small dice

FULL LIFE CYCLE GREENHOUSE GAS EMISSIONS FOR COMMON FOODS

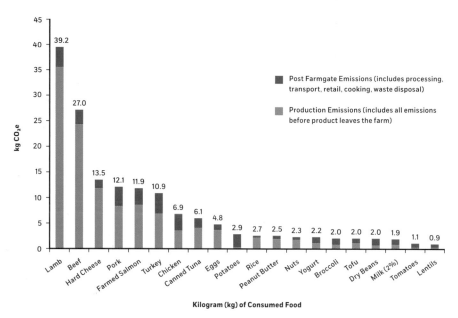

SOURCE: THE ENVIRONMENTAL WORKING GROUP

The chart above shows the life cycle total of greenhouse gas emissions for common protein foods and vegetables, expressed as kilograms (kg) of carbon dioxide equivalents (CO_2e) per kg of consumed product.

Key Findings from the Life Cycle Assessments

Lamb, beef, and cheese have the highest emissions. This is true, in part, because they come from ruminant animals that constantly generate methane through their digestive process, called enteric fermentation. Methane (CH_4)—a greenhouse gas twenty-five times more potent than carbon dioxide (CO_2)—accounts for nearly half the emissions generated in this study's Nebraska beef production model (see chart). Pound for pound, ruminant animals also require significantly more energy-intensive feed and generate more manure than pork or chicken (see figure).

Lamb has the greatest impact, generating 86.4 lb/39.2 kg of carbon dioxide equivalents (CO_2e) for each kg eaten—about 50 percent more than beef. While beef and lamb generate comparable amounts of methane and require similar quantities of feed, lamb generates

more emissions per kg in part because it produces less edible meat relative to the sheep's live weight. Since just 1 percent of the meat consumed by Americans is lamb, however, it contributes very little to overall U.S. greenhouse gas emissions.

Beef has the second-highest emissions, generating 59.6 lb/27.0 kg of CO_2e per kg consumed. That's more than twice the emissions of pork, nearly four times that of chicken, and more than thirteen times that of vegetable proteins such as beans, lentils, and tofu. About 30 percent of the meat consumed in America is beef.

Cheese generates the third-highest emissions, 29.7 lb/13.5 kg of CO_2e per kg eaten, so vegetarians who eat a lot of dairy aren't off the hook. Less-dense cheese (such as cottage) results in fewer greenhouse gases since it takes less milk to produce it.

Copyright © Environmental Working Group, www.ewg.org. Reprinted with permission.

ACKNOWLEDGMENTS

We want to thank so many people who helped make our cookbook so wonderful. Chef Jesse Cool, a pioneer in the world of sustainable food, introduced us to Bill LeBlond, executive editor of cookbooks at Chronicle Books, who championed our concept of "vegan food for everyone." We are grateful to him, and all the very smart and talented folks at Chronicle Books who were part of our team, including Doug Ogan, managing editor; Marie Oishi, assistant managing editor; Brooke Johnson, senior designer; Steve Kim, senior production coordinator; Peter Perez, associate marketing director; and David Hawk, publicist. We'd especially like to thank Amy Treadwell, senior editor, who guided this whole process with much expertise and patience.

We feel extremely lucky to have had the privilege of collaborating with incredible photographer Sara Remington, who is responsible for the stunning photos that brought our produce and recipes to life. We also want to thank her very talented team: Sarah Cave, prop stylist; Constance Pikulas, food stylist; Kassandra Medeiros, camera assistant; and Chelsey Bawot, food preparation. And we send a big thank-you to Janna Jo Williams, our very gifted farm-stand garden and event manager, who generously assisted with all of the Carmel Valley photo shoots.

Pam McKinstry tested almost all of our recipes and has been a great mentor. Sarah LaCasse, Earthbound Farm's executive chef, contributed fantastic recipes and creative ideas (like green olives in our barley side dish). Ashley Koff, RD, shared her vast expertise about food and nutrition, and two brilliant writers, Laura Davis and our dear friend Darryle Pollack, helped finesse and improve our copy.

There are many people at Earthbound Farm to thank. We greatly appreciate all the time Christopher Thomas spent creating nutritional analyses for our recipes. Thanks to Hillary Fish, Samantha Cabaluna, and Charles Sweat for their support, and to all of Earthbound Farm's employees, partners, and farmers that work so hard to bring delicious organic produce to our kitchen, and to families around the country.

We feel very blessed to have such a wonderful community of family and close friends who have supported us during this project with their love, enthusiasm, and recipe feedback. Hugs and kisses to you all! Our deep appreciation to Hilary Nichols for helping us harmonize our work styles and find the magic in creating a cookbook as a mother-daughter team, and to our vegan friend Angela Hains, for her huge enthusiasm for our recipes just when we needed it most.

We are especially grateful to Jeffrey Goodman, fabulous son/brother, who joyfully ate large quantities of the recipes we were testing, reassuring us repeatedly that young men who usually choose steak for dinner could be perfectly happy with our vegan dishes. Thanks, too, Jeffrey, for your valuable feedback and suggestions throughout. And last, but the very opposite of least, we both want to thank Drew Goodman, amazing husband/father, for the countless generous ways you supported this project. We all know that your palate is the best in the family, and we thank you for helping us improve and perfect so many of these recipes. We adore both of you more than words can say!

—MYRA & MAREA

INDEX

3 1901 05812 2054